To
a Rising Sun

GOD, THE GOSPEL, AND YOUR LIFE IN THIS AGE

STEPHANIE QUICK

To Trace a Rising Sun: God, the Gospel, and Your Life in This Age
By Stephanie Quick
Copyright © 2018 FAI Publishing

All rights reserved. No part of this publication may be reproduced, stored in a retrieval system or transmitted in any form or by any means, electronic, mechanical, photocopying, recording or otherwise without the prior permission of the publisher or in accordance with the provisions of the Copyright, Designs and Patents Act 1988 or under the terms of any licence permitting limited copying issued by the Copyright Licensing Agency.

Unless marked otherwise, Scripture quotations are from The Holy Bible, English Standard Version® (ESV®), Copyright © 2001 by Crossway, a publishing ministry of Good News Publishers. Used by permission. All rights reserved.

All italics within quotations have been added by this Author for emphasis, unless otherwise indicated in a footnote. In addition, some personal pronouns in Scripture have been capitalized by the Author.

Cover design: Stephanie Quick
Cover image: Marc Ash
Interior book design: Lala England

A CIP record for this book is available from the Library of Congress Cataloging-in-Publication Data

ISBN-13: 978-1-67112-145-4

"For I will not venture to speak of anything except what Christ has accomplished through me to bring the Gentiles to obedience—by word and deed, by the power of signs and wonders, by the power of the Spirit of God—so that from Jerusalem and all the way around to Illyricum I have fulfilled the ministry of the gospel of Christ; and **thus I make it my ambition to preach the gospel, not where Christ has already been named, lest I build on someone else's foundation**, but as it is written, 'those who have never been told of Him will see, and those who have never heard will understand.'"

Romans 15:18–21

CONTENTS

Preface vii

SECTION ONE

Preeminent in All Things 3
Tracing the Dawn 5

SECTION TWO

Knowledge Alive 13
The Beautiful Name 17
Merciful Magnification 23

SECTION THREE

The Beautiful Son 31
The Lord Will Provide Himself 35
All Things 41

SECTION FOUR

Grace Personified, the Word Incarnate 49
A Type of Him Who Was to Come 53
A Suitable Companion 61
Deceit and Edenic Gravedigging 65
The Washing Word 73

SECTION FIVE

The Blood-Soaked Garden 85
Sober Responsibility 89
Intercede (v): to Intervene 95
That Others May Live 101
Manifold Wisdom 105
Gethsemanes and Golgothas 113

SECTION SIX

Days & Darkness 119
Made and Allowed to Understand 123
Watching Weather 127
Our Blessed Hope 133
Something Like Jasper 137

SECTION SEVEN

Occupy Till I Come 143
Work that Survives Fire 149
A Unique Confrontation 155
Elevating or Emulating 161
The Wisest Waste 165

APPENDIX

I Never Made a Sacrifice 175
acknowledgments 177
about the author 179
about fai 179

Preface

THIS IS NOT A TYPICAL BOOK.

This book has existed in some form for a decade now, from notes to outlines and drafts, rewrites and revisions. It has outlived hard drives and journeyed with me from the American Midwest, to the South Pacific, to the mountainous border region between Iraq and Iran, and throughout the Middle East.

Much like the physical act of "tracing" a subject with line and lead, writing this has been, for me, a process of revisiting, meditating, and marinating in prized and precious truths in a way that let Truth reveal more to, and—often—confront me. These chapters and essays echo the convictions that have shaped my adult life and informed every major decision I've made since graduating high school. There is one consistent story between the first words of Genesis and the last words of Revelation—"let there be light"[1] and "let it be (amen)"[2]—that, for all its cosmic and macro objectivity, bears every weight on the breath in your specific lungs the moment you—you—read this. I believe the form now in your hand is my best shape of this sketch.

My prayer for these pages is that they bring you into deeper waters of the eternal Word with something of a holistic vantage of all the words borne by the prophets, patriarchs, apostles, and psalmists. It is my humble commentary on the story of this broken, beautiful, and redemptive age in eternity.

---

1 Genesis 1:3
2 Revelation 22:21

You will not find "10 of" anything—there are no lists or self-help steps between the preface and conclusion. This does not end with an application. It is more abstract than linear, but it has been written with diligent intention. I ask you for your patience through the pages, and I've included every footnote I can fathom to offer bunny trails to wander down. Let us all get lost in the Scriptures.

because Jesus –
Stephanie Quick
Mediterranean Basin
November 2018

Section One

To Trace a Rising Sun

"Well can I trace the dawn, the rise, and the progress of any feeble Missionary Spirit that I have to the readings, conversations, and essays called for by the student Missionary Association in St. Andrews."

Alexander Duff, 1831

CHAPTER ONE

PREEMINENT IN ALL THINGS

THE BELIEVERS IN COLOSSAE HAD DEVIATED. A long stone's throw from the thriving community in Ephesus—the only community to not receive a corrective letter from the apostle Paul—the Colossians had begun to get muddy with their Christology.[1] Paul wrote to clear up the water in their well. Unlike the Galatians, who got lost along the way of the Gospel's implications,[2] the Colossians got confused on the centerpiece of the Gospel itself. Rather, Himself. They got confused about Jesus.

His letter opens with brief greetings, a short prayer, and then a loaded exposition of who Jesus is, laying a powerful ultimatum before Colossian Christians: Jesus is either everything the prophets, apostles and He Himself say He is, or He is nothing at all. As Charles Spurgeon so simply put it, "If Christ be anything, He must be everything."[3]

He must be.

This is why—and only how—the Gospel has such explosive implications. This is why Golgotha is of cosmic consequence. If He is anything, He is everything—or nothing at all. He is the image of the

---

1   USCCB. "Letter to the Colossians." Accessed September 11, 2016. http://www.usccb.org/bible/colossians/0.
2   See the letter to the Galatians
3   Charles H. Spurgeon, "Christ is All" (1871). Accessed September 11, 2016. http://www.spurgeon.org/sermons/1006.php

invisible God, and thus supreme and sovereign over everything.[4] He can thus demand preeminence and deserve the highest Name in all the heavens, earth and everything under the earth.[5] He will forever receive the unadulterated worship of every creature.[6] Every knee will bow to Him. Every tongue will confess His Lordship.[7] Worship is a unique gift in this age of "believing without seeing."[8] It will be quite different when the Son of Man is exalted in His glory while all our thoughts, intents and secret things are laid bare for every eye to see.[9]

In this way, Paul could hinge the legitimacy of Christian discipleship on the resurrection of the saints upon the Lord's appearance at the end of the age. If we are not resurrected, this whole thing is a farce and there's no one on earth more pathetic than our lot.[10] Why? Because Jesus said He is the Resurrection.[11] If He isn't, He isn't anything else He claimed to be either and we should all go home. If Christ be anything, He must be everything.

The age-ending Day of the LORD will expose every wicked thing and reveal every holy mystery kept hidden from our eyes until then. The "Desire of the Nations"[12] will be seen in full splendor, and all our questions will evaporate with the sin which so easily and dreadfully ensnares us. The "Branch of the LORD" so faithfully and graciously extended to a bloodthirsty humanity will be seen for all He is—beautiful, glorious, and worth everything we gave Him while we had it in our hands to offer.[13] We will not dread eternity with Him. We will not resent His reign. We will not resist His hand. The dim mirrors removed and shattered, our eyes will see Him fully and clearly. Adoration will erupt from our hearts and rush from our lips: "You are everything You said and more."

Put simply, "You're everything."

Nothing else will matter.

---

4   See Colossians 1:15–20
5   See Philippians 2:9–10
6   See Revelation 5
7   See Philippians 2:10–11
8   See John 20:29
9   See Romans 2:16
10   See 1 Corinthians 15:16–20
11   See John 11:25
12   Haggai 2:7
13   Isaiah 4:2

CHAPTER TWO

TRACING THE DAWN

When I was twelve years old, I heard an Indian-American couple share their story at Calvary Chapel in the States. My family was new to the Protestant circuit, having just begun to step away from the Catholic community (which is to say nothing against the Catholic community; this was just my journey), and these folks were the first "missionaries" I'd encountered. I may not have even heard the term before—and my first impression was bleak. *You sold your house to do what? Move back to India? Isn't it hot there? You did what with your red sports car?! ...I wish I had a red sports car...*

I spent my tumultuous high school years in a thriving youth ministry run by a church not far from my house. It was led by good people who love Jesus and love His Word. They're still in my life, and I'm so grateful for them. Yet I still nearly became a statistic—"one of those" kids who leave high school, leave youth group, stop going to church and get their worldview from their Twitter feed. We could see it coming even then; evangelical paragroups had already done the research to empirically prove what we could ourselves clearly observe. Most of our American youth group disciples were leaving the church at eighteen and falling away by the time they were twenty. If they're anything like me, they were trying to make sense of the point of everything. Nobody wants to waste their time. Even fools spend their lives on what they think is wise. Good leadership can't save us (helpful as it is), and the inch-deep faith of immaturity can't plumb line us for the long haul. We had—and have—questions, and we needed—and need—answers that can stand up to the full force and fury of our tensions and doubt. And at some point, we need to grow up and own our confrontation with truth and lies. We need to know where we land and stand in the bigger picture. And we *really* need to know Jesus.

Maybe you're reading this and you're older than I am. Maybe you're wondering what to do with the twilight of your life in this age. Maybe you're in high school or college and you're wondering what the point is, wondering what to do with all the decades ahead of you. Maybe you're wondering what to do with the Bible, and how to make sense of it all. Wondering why we live in this age with all these stories and all our promises and limitations, all our dreams and all our handicaps. Wondering what Jesus really has to do with anything. Wondering if He's better than a hot ride. Consider this: one day you'll be old (either in this age or in eternity), and you'll look back over your life and have the luxury of retrospect to discern the decisions you made. Even the bad ones. And you will, with certainty, stand before Jesus one day. You will either mourn your missed opportunities to love Him well in this age or you will celebrate every sacrifice with new clarity on how trivial everything else was in light of who He is. We will all reckon with how we reconciled and resolved ourselves to this question: *What is Jesus worth?*

When Alexander Duff reflected on his life in 1831, he'd by then spent decades in ministry in India. He was staring into the twilight years of his life on this side of time, and he knew it. As he looked behind him, he remembered the vibrant life of a young, healthy, intelligent man with all the world before him, and he remembered when he packed his bags. He remembered when and why he made the decision to board a ship to India. He remembered why he stayed every time a ship sailed east. As an old man, he recounted:

> *"Well can I trace the dawn, the rise, and the progress of any feeble missionary spirit that I have to the readings,*

conversations, and essays called for by the student Missionary Association in St. Andrews."[1]

Duff was part of a group remembered as the "St. Andrews Six." He and a handful of his buddies helped found and give leadership to a student society committed to funding missionaries from the United Kingdom to the unreached and unengaged areas of the world—at a time when people became missionaries kind of because they couldn't be trusted to do anything else. It was not regarded as a dignified position, and the resources given to it (in both money and manpower) reflected that. But Duff and his friends were provoked by men like William Carey, who'd sailed to the other side of the world to tell people who didn't know about Jesus about Jesus. They dug into the Scriptures, read a bunch of missionary biographies, prayed together, ate together, and wrestled through it all together. Many of them concluded the burden of responsibility for stewarding the Good News of the Gospel of the Kingdom fell upon them simply because they were members and ambassadors of the Kingdom. None felt *called* to preach or pioneer. They just couldn't shake the testimony of the Word of God that *Jesus was worth it and the unreached deserve it.*

It's not that I think missionaries are the only true Christians. It's just that I think *Jesus is worth it and the unreached deserve it.* This is not a book about missions. This is a book about the beauty and worth of Jesus.

So we have to talk about missions.

With only 0.005% of Christians serving as missionaries to unreached peoples, and only 0.1% of the global evangelical income given to missions— and with just 1% of *that* presently given to efforts on the frontier[2]—I have a hunch I'm not the only one with a bleak first impression of global missions. We love our square footage and red sports cars. But if statistics reveal anything, most Christians meet their Maker with that bleak impression. And if Scripture tells us anything, the Day of the LORD will fact-check us all.[3]

---

[1] Piggin, Stuart, and John Roxborogh. *The St. Andrews Seven: The Finest Flowering of Missionary Zeal in Scottish History.* Edinburgh [etc.]: Banner of Truth Trust, 2015, p. 48

[2] The Traveling Team. "General Statistics." http://thetravelingteam.org/stats. Accessed 16 February 2015.

[3] Isaiah 2:12–22; 4:2; Romans 2:5–8; 3:19; I Corinthians 3:10–15; 4:4b–5; II Timothy 4:1; I Peter 4:5; Revelation 22:12

At the risk of a cliché, the world looks a bit different than it did a few years ago. The Syrian Civil War was, at the time, just another conflict emerging out of the Arab Spring—nothing to be said for genocide, chemical warfare, or the splintered bodies of children in the rubble of ancient cities. Osama bin Laden had been tossed in frigid waters, and a bunch of drunk college kids who were learning how to read when 9/11 happened danced in the streets of D.C.. The American Church squabbled a bit over Chick-Fil-A and Duck Dynasty controversies—and had the audacity to call the backlash "persecution."

Even then, the term "10/40 Window" was a buzzword in the evangelical subculture. Even then, there were gaping holes in the Great Commission. Even then, millions bookended their lives with breaths devoid the name of Jesus. Even then, minarets summoned the 1.6 billion Muslims alive today to bow their knee to a god who can neither see them nor hear their prayers—*five times a day.*

We in the West weren't confronted then with street bombs, cafe sieges, or YouTube terrorism. We weren't confronted with black-clad jihadis launching a production company to showcase their slaughters to the world. In our bubble, brutal scourges were in history books, and the post-modern world had evolved to democratic "coexistence." We're a few generations removed from the collapse of the Ottoman Empire, and no one taught us the term "caliphate" in grade school. Westerners professing the name of Jesus weren't confronted with faces of men, women and children who have never heard His Name. We weren't confronted with angry nations who've heard a distortion of the Gospel at best, or with our self-preserving reluctance to bear them a witness worthy of the Name we claim.

We are now.

Generations are "justified" by what they give birth to.[4] Our children will bear testimony on that Day—did it bother us that He was blasphemed? Did it bother us that lives were born and buried without ever being given witness of the Kingdom? Did it bother us that two thousand years after His ascension, we avoided unreached households because we feared their hostility? Will they inherit apathy, or will they meet our King with expectations of His majesty and worth because we taught them every sacrifice is insignificant compared to His glory?

---

4   Matthew 11:19

When we were uniquely confronted with a Christless world, how did we respond—were we willing to gamble the Great Commission against our volatile 401(k)?

Duff's testimony affirms the fact that we have to understand the story. We have to understand who Jesus is, what He is doing, and where we fit in the narrative. What rights do we have? What responsibilities do we bear?

I believe it would serve us well to know the story—to borrow Duff's words and "trace the sun," so to speak.

It's been several years since I scorned the testimony of those Christ-exalting laborers, and but a few since I first stepped foot on Muslim-majority soil. Western churches are still full of twelve year olds wondering if Jesus is better than all their other options, all their other desires. I pray someone will tell them with their lives that He is. Western nations are still full of believers grappling with the implications of the fact that He is—better than legitimate pleasures, better than sins, better than blasphemies.

If He is, it is fundamentally unjust that He is scorned across the earth.

If He is, He changes everything.

Let goods, kindred and red sports cars go.[5]

---

5   This line is a wordplay on Martin Luther's "A Mighty Fortress" hymn:

   Let goods and kindred go
   This mortal life also
   The body they may kill
   God's truth abideth still

SECTION TWO

DAWN TILL DUSK

*"From the rising of the sun to its setting
My Name will be great among the nations."*

MALACHI 1:11

CHAPTER THREE

KNOWLEDGE ALIVE

"BEHOLD; GOD IS GREAT, AND WE DO NOT KNOW HIM."[1] Just as it takes God to love God,[2] so we need Him to know Him as well. Eden's trees identified our need for knowledge; our choice of their fruits exposed our inability to seek or steward knowledge responsibly. As creatures of the Creator, we require revelation of the One without origin and such knowledge, accordingly, cannot originate with us. We are neither the authors nor the governors of eternity, yet it is squarely and surely set within our hearts, daily provoking us to grapple for what we can feel but cannot see.[3] If we are but walking mirrors, we must know the Image we bear to know ourselves with any measure of clarity;[4] indeed, self-knowledge cannot exist without such. When we encounter Him who inhabits eternity,[5] we gain the kind of revelatory knowledge—wisdom—that can shape and inform our daily decisions to such a degree that our lives and legacies are crafted around who He is and what He is about. Our "best lives" hinge on our congruent knowledge with the One who knows our frames,

---

1 Job 36:26
2 1 John 4:19
3 See Ecclesiastes 3:11
4 Genesis 1:26–28; 2:7
5 See Isaiah 57:15

orchestrates our futures, and hears every thought racing through our minds.[6] We have nothing apart from Him.[7]

Paul petitioned the generous God to "enlighten the eyes of [our] understanding"[8] to give us a leg up to comprehend the Incomprehensible. If "it is the glory of God to conceal a matter, but the glory of kings to search it out,"[9] and He has promised to respond generously to those who take up the quest,[10] let us hear the invitation to seek His face and respond with a diligent and unwavering "yes."[11] His Word illuminates our paths,[12] so as we seek Him, we see more clearly—we see ourselves, our lives, our callings, and our communities more clearly. What we believe to be true about Jesus bears every weight and shape of our daily decisions, lifestyle choices, and patterns of thought. Whether or not the truth of Christ breaks into the darkness of our idolatrous minds is literally life or death to our souls[13]—and those of people around us. "It is for freedom Christ has set us free,"[14] and knowing Jesus is what turns the lights on to liberate us from the dark cages of accusation and unbelief.

Our Son of Man appeared to destroy the works of the devil and offer eternal life—"life abundant"—to those who call upon His Name. Again, we are brought back to the primacy and preeminence of His Name. This age isn't about our salvation. It is about the revelation of the God who saves. To know His Name is to know who He is and what He is like. It is to know Him. Knowing Him brings us back to life. Knowing Him restores heartbeats to walking corpses and injects purpose into our pulses. We are made for Him, through Him, and by Him; in His Image and for His purposes.[15] In knowing Him, we meet, find, and mine out our truest selves.

The integrity of the Word of God and infallible nature of His Personhood informs our lives with such decree and directive that our

---

6   John 10:10
7   John 15:5
8   Ephesians 1:18
9   Proverbs 25:2
10 See Jeremiah 29:13
11 See Psalm 27:8
12 See Psalm 119:105
13 See Hosea 4:6; John 17:3; Colossians 2:3
14 Galatians 5:1
15 Colossians 1:15–20

legacies themselves are shaped therein. In the words of the apostle, while we are limited on this side of time and space by dim sight of eternity, we will one day see by glorious light in full.[16] Despite our limitations, we yet become what we behold.[17] It is imperative, then, that we behold the Person of Jesus as revealed through every page of Scripture from beginning to end. What we discover about Him will orient our lives around His light like planets around the blazing sun; inevitably, revelation of who He is will lead us to make decisions that don't make sense unless we will be raised from the dead.

A young woman from a small town realized Jesus was the Lord of the Resurrection, and it changed everything for her. She knew that kind of Lordship would cost Him everything, and she worshipped Him for it with means that cost her everything.[18] This is the kind of discipleship we're destined for.[19] This is the kind of all-in affection, outright obedience, and unflinching allegiance He is due—and this is the only way to make sense of the hearts now beating in our chests. "If Christ be anything, He must be everything." Knowing Him is life, ransoming us from the blasphemous death knells we instinctively buy into.

It's only fair that everybody hears this gloriously good news. The God of Israel has been committed to the international intention of the Everlasting Covenant since before He called Abram out of Ur.[20] This is why ownership of the Gospel bears an obligation to share the Gospel.[21] Paul knew this, and it drove him to the far corners of the Roman Empire.[22] This is why Gospel poverty and blasphemy are two sides of the same unjust coin. Jesus is worth being unequivocally worshipped, and every human made by His hand in His Image deserves to hear His Name.

His Name is our only means of eternal life.[23]

---

16   See 1 Corinthians 13:12
17   See 2 Corinthians 3:18
18   Matthew 26:6–13
19   Matthew 26:13
20   See Genesis 11:31–12:4
21   Romans 1:14–17
22   Romans 15:19–21
23   Joel 2:32; Romans 10:13

CHAPTER FOUR

The Beautiful Name

"Then men began to call upon the name of the Lord."[1] It took a few generations and a handful of massive blunders and moral failures, but we did it. We came to the end of our rope and realized we cannot author our own redemption and hope. We needed (and need) Jesus. By the time the two who bought the snake's lie met their first grandson, mankind finally began to pray—we finally began to "call upon the name of the Lord" and appeal to everything we know to be true about who He is and what He is like. We must, therefore, know His name—not just the phonetic sound He goes by like we need something to catch the attention of our friend across the room—but what He is known for and identified by. His name is His nature. His name is His character. His name is His personality. His name is who He is. "Calling upon" His name is not simply a summons; we do not pray to get His attention. Scripture tells us we already have it. We pray to pry our white knuckles off control of our own lives and cast ourselves headlong into the caring and controlling hands that took the nails that had our names on them at the Place of the Skull.

When we think something about someone that is not true about them, it is a misunderstanding. It could be the fruit of jaded presumption

---

[1] Genesis 4:26, NKJV

and sometimes is incredibly unfair. When we think something that is not true about the LORD who Himself is Truth, it is more than a misunderstanding—it's an injustice. He is the truth and light that gives us life; believing something false about the Holy One engages with idolatry and entertains ideas that lead to death.[2] At a minimum, we owe it to ourselves to believe things that are true, deny ideas that are false, and educate ourselves well enough to know the difference.

The LORD of glory, who dwells in unapproachable light,[3] has not left us in the dark. He's given us an extensive explanation of who He is and what He is doing in His written word. We are not without counsel, and hold more resources of revelation in our hands than the sons of Adam's exile did any time we hold a Bible. In this way, we have every reason to marvel at the mercy and grace given to us in Jesus: that Heaven would give untrustworthy traitors so prone to love lies the stewardship of something as precious as the Scriptures. We cannot go a day without the possibility of thinking something untrue or saying something false. He meets us with His Word anyway. He meets us with His truth because He is merciful.

Reiterated throughout the words between the "In the beginning" of Genesis 1:1 and the final "Amen" of Revelation 22:21 is the undergirding point and purpose to this age and our lives: all things are "for His name's sake."[4] All things are His, and all things are for Him.[5] David asked for forgiveness not because he deserved to receive it, but for His name's sake.[6] Moses begged for mercy not because the golden calf incident gave him a leg to stand on, but for His name's sake.[7] Daniel leaned on the covenantal integrity and future glory of Jerusalem not because Jerusalem *deserved* (then or now) to be known for the LORD's righteousness, but for His name's sake.[8] The apostles fought for doctrinal integrity not because they liked to argue about theology, but because they cared about the name of Jesus being defined and

---

2   Tozer, A.W. *The Knowledge of the Holy*, (1961). New York: HarperCollins. p. 1.

3   See 1 Timothy 6:16

4   See 1 Samuel 12:22; Psalm 23:3; 25:11; 31:3; 79:9; 106:8; 109:21; 143:11; Isaiah 48:9; 66:5; Jeremiah 14:7,21; Ezekiel 20:44; Matthew 10:22; 19:29; 24:9; Mark 13:13; Luke 21:12,17; 1 John 2:12; Revelation 2:3

5   See Colossians 1:15-20

6   See Psalm 25:11

7   See Exodus 33:12-16

8   See Daniel 9:19

represented *rightly*. The apostolic burden is to bear the integrity of the Name of the LORD—*for His name's sake*. They scattered their lives to the four winds in surrounding nations for His name's sake. Not for theirs. Never for ours. For His name's sake, and His alone. When all is said and done, there will be one sound resounding through the corridors of the ages: the name of Jesus.

We will need eternity to worship Him, because we will need eternity to get to know Him. We'll still never see or hear or know everything about Him. We will be endlessly intrigued, endlessly fascinated, and endlessly satisfied in Him. He is as beautiful and mysterious as He is dynamic, and it has taken this age just to begin to see something of His mercy. His redemption. His unflinching commitment to covenant. His gracious patience. His joyful servanthood. His offensive advocacy for His enemies.

There are conversations and encounters recorded in Scripture wherein someone learned something new about the LORD, and they then began to call Him by a new name. They'd refer to Him differently because their revelation had grown beyond their prior language. He is *limitless* and our language is not. Our rhetoric will bind our tongues. Relying on it will bind our hearts. Our songs will fall short, for choruses cannot contain Him. We can know all the answers for Sunday school quizzes and "do all the stuff" of spiritual disciples and still not know His name. It's important that we familiarize ourselves with these moments in the biblical witness (and we will, briefly, in the next chapter), and devote investments of time and energy into prayerful meditation on what He reveals about Himself, anchored in the infallible texts of the Judeo-Christian Scriptures. We need to know Jesus. We need to know His nature. We need to know His character well enough to refute accusations against Him. We will live through so many Genesis 3 "but did God really say?" moments in this age, and we will die (like our ancestors in Eden)[9] if we cannot answer with clear minds and confident hearts: "It is *written*."[10]

---

9   See Genesis 2:17

10 In Matthew 4, Jesus experiences three temptations from the enemy while fasting in the wilderness. All of the devil's offers were grounded in a distortion of Scripture; Jesus was able to discern and resist with Scriptural clarity. His is the example for us.

What we'll find as we immerse ourselves in the biblical narrative and revelation of Jesus is how altogether "other" He is. Truly, there is none like Him. It is only worth the effort to exalt His name if His name is actually worth exalting—if He is actually as unique and "other-than" as His claimed holiness describes. Scripture testifies that He is. The testimony of the "great cloud of witnesses" is that He is. In my own life, I can say as somebody who has banked everything on the integrity of His Word, He is everything He says He is. His Word is as true and reliable as He claims. He has the incredible foresight, clear leadership, and authoritative control His sovereignty necessitates. He is, in fact, the "Good Shepherd."[11] He is, in fact, the Way, the Truth, and the Life.[12] He is the God who sees and hears and knows.[13] He is the God who provides.[14] He is the One who heals.[15] He is the Mighty One.[16] He is the "chief upholder of my soul."[17] He is the "wonderful counselor," almost better translated as the "strategic military commander."[18] His is the goodness and mercy that hounds us down and finds us out.[19] He is the Everlasting Father,[20] the Father of lights,[21] Father of glory.[22] He is just and the justifier of those who believe.[23] He is the God of the living,[24] the God who raises the dead.[25] He is Jesus Christ the Righteous,[26] the beginning and the end, the Almighty.[27] Sometimes it is enough to say, very simply, that He just is.[28]

In Judges 13, the couple who would become Samson's parents were visited by the Angel of the LORD—twice. The accounts of their

---

11   John 10:11-18
12   John 14:6
13   Genesis 16:13; 2 Chronicles 16:9; Isaiah 59:1; 66:2
14   Genesis 22:14; Matthew 6:25-34; 1 Timothy 6:17
15   Exodus 15:26
16   Genesis 49:24; Joshua 22:22; Psalm 50:1; 132:2,5; Isaiah 1:24; 49:26; 60:16
17   Psalm 54:4; Motyer, A. *Psalms by the day: A new devotional translation*, (2016). Tain: Christian Focus.
18   Isaiah 9:6
19   Psalm 23:6
20   Isaiah 9:6
21   James 1:17
22   Ephesians 1:17
23   Romans 3:26
24   Mark 12:27; Luke 20:38
25   John 11:25-26; 2 Corinthians 4:14; Hebrews 11:19
26   1 John 2:1
27   Revelation 21:6; 22:13
28   Hebrews 11:6

exchanges are one of the lesser-known gems hidden within Scripture, but it is a wildly unique and incredible story. There are scholastic debates about who or what the "Angel of the LORD" is in Scripture, but a good rule of thumb is that angels never allow a man to worship them. It was the Angel of the LORD who appeared to Moses in the burning bush and advised the man to remove his shoes; Joshua followed suit in the desert outside of Jericho and was not rebuked; John attempted to do so with a lesser angel and was promptly corrected.[29] Manoah and his wife, then barren, were met by and received prophetic promises from the Angel of the LORD, and as they gave Him a burnt offering, they asked Him His name. I tell this story now because I want His response to echo through our hearts and minds as we explore the worth, virtue, and exaltation of His name in our lives, homes, communities, and nations:

"Why do you ask My name, seeing it is wonderful?"[30]

May Jesus "enlighten the eyes of our understanding"[31] so that we can see that His name is wonderful and worth it all. May the Holy Spirit make much of Him in our hearts. May the Father of lights and glory become our absolute preoccupation. May we fall in love with our Maker to depths and degrees we don't deserve. Let us fall headlong into the saving knowledge of the One who shepherds and sanctifies us at such great cost to Himself without hesitation or second thought. May we love Jesus for Jesus, because Jesus.

---

29 See Exodus 3:1-6; Joshua 5:14-15; Revelation 22:9
30 Judges 13:18
31 Ephesians 1:18

CHAPTER FIVE

Merciful Magnification

THIS AGE IS A PLAY; THE COSMOS IS THE STAGE, and Jesus has cast Himself in the starring role. He gets to put Himself in the center; He is destined and deserves to be "preeminent in all things."[1] We are revived and renewed and resurrected by knowing Him, by knowing "the Life."[2] His own persistent self-exaltation is sacrificial, in that it is in our best interests and has cost Him all but everything. No mind of man could imagine a God who gives all to His enemies—including, but not limited to, His life; Jesus' lifelong giving of Himself gave light to our darkness, and "in [His] light, we see light."[3] His costly love ransoms us from darkness and transfers us "into the kingdom of the Son of His love."[4] Thus the magnification and fame of His Name is the most merciful means to a magnificent end. Our own sin, every one a betrayal against our Sovereign, bars us from the privilege of hearing His Name. We cannot *earn* the right to know what He is like. We *get* to because He is good and His goodness is for our own good. Dawn first struck darkness in the Genesis *so that* man would grapple and come to know our Maker, and create a cruciform witness

---

1   Colossians 1:18
2   John 14:6; 17:3
3   Psalm 36:9
4   Colossians 1:13

of the Image we bear for all the powers of the air to see.[5] No part or portion of human history is an accident; nothing about this world is an alternative to what Eden couldn't be—Jesus does not have need for Plan Bs. Every era and epoch is wrought with intention and sovereign orchestration.

When the man from Ur was called to walk until he was told to stop, the LORD had every nation in mind: "All nations of the earth will be blessed."[6] To that end, He made a specific nation; a firstborn of sorts, identified by circumcision and covenantal peculiarity. Abraham's son and grandson would carry a holy mantle none deserved, sacrificially displaying the God who does as He pleases from the earliest call of the patriarch to modern day. Their election would offend the world and burden them with sanctification and sacrificial witness: the "Servant Nation" would bear the Image of the Suffering Servant until Kingdom come, and the brunt of man's rage against the holy covenant until it comes in full.[7] Yet as mercy does, it clings to the love that bears and hopes and endures and believes: when Abraham's dream comes to full fruition, when the scores of his children will inherit the fullness of the land promised yet seen by neither the patriarchs nor Moses, a beautiful song will have soaked into the soil of the nations. When the Son of David inherits his throne, He will be welcomed with a melody that erupted from Jerusalem so long ago, traveled to the ends of the earth, and made its way back again to the City of the Great King: "Blessed is He who comes in the Name of the LORD!"[8]

In the Name of the LORD.

Indeed, "let the nations be glad."[9] Some generations after Jacob's sons reached the end of their Egyptian Exodus, and a few longer still since Abraham was first called out of the Chaldeans, the early apostles stood on the Mount of Olives with the risen Son of David and asked Him one pertinent and burning question: "Lord, will You now restore the Kingdom to Israel?"[10] They were not without reason to wonder if

---

5   Ephesians 3:8–12
6   Genesis 12:3; 22:18; 26:4
7   See Daniel 11:30
8   See Psalm 118:26; Isaiah 24:14–16; 42:10–16; Matthew 23:39; Luke 19:3
9   Psalm 67:4
10 Acts 1:6

they were living in what Daniel described as "the time of the end,"[11] but it was a mistaken perception. "Timing isn't yours to know," said the Lord; for now, "you will be My witnesses in Jerusalem, and in all Judea and Samaria, and to the end of the earth."[12] The apostles were thus commissioned as walking mirrors to the farthest reaches of the earth—like Abraham, "walk until you can't walk any further"—until He returns "in the same way [they] saw Him go into heaven;"[13] in this way, the apostolic witness of "this Gospel of the Kingdom"[14] to the very end of the earth is meant to spread and sustain an incarnate message of the Incarnate God until, in both time and space, this earth reaches its appointed end.[15]

Every Jewish ear listening to Jesus that day, in the moments before His Ascension, would've recognized the phrase "the ends of the earth." David sang about them.[16] Isaiah and Jeremiah both wrote at length about them.[17] Their role and presence in the prophetic Hebrew texts is both distinct and uniquely yoked to the "new song,"[18] a concept deeply woven into the coming Day of the LORD. This new song responds to the revelation of God's saving arm and righteousness in Christ Jesus. It is worship undergirded by the apostolic witness to this Gospel of the Kingdom—meaning, the doctrines are true blue Bible. It hasn't deviated from Scripture, yet responds afresh to the dawning light of the revelation of God—to the very hearing and understanding of His Name; who He is, what He is like, and why He is doing what He is doing. Isaiah wrote of islands as far away from the center of the earth as one could go, where light first breaks over sandy shores and seas, specifically magnifying the "God of Israel," "giving glory to the [very] name of the LORD."[19] The prophet described a "new song" coming from the very end of the earth.

---

11   Daniel 8:19; 11:35,40; 12:1–9
12   Acts 1:8
13   Acts 1:11
14   See Matthew 24:14
15   See Revelation 21:1
16   See Psalm 2:8; 22:27; 48:10; 59:13; 65:5,8; 67:7; 72:8; 98:3
17   Isaiah 5:26; 24:14–16; 40:28; 41:5,9; 42:10; 45:22; 49:6; 52:10; Jeremiah 10:13; 16:19; 25:31; 51:16
18   Psalm 33:3; 40:3; 96:1; 98:1; 144:9; 149:1; Isaiah 42:10; Revelation 5:9; 14:3
19   Isaiah 24:14–16

Delivering the message of the melody is the crux—pun intended—of the Great Commission given to the apostles and Body of Jesus. We're to reach the ends of the earth until the LORD appears and this earth ends and is made anew.[20] That is our task until the "restoration of all things."[21] This message launched by the Great King from His City in the center of the world[22] is to reach these furthest coasts and, per the prophet Isaiah and affirmation of Jesus, make its way back again. This is the phase we're in now. When our "strategic commander"[23] gave these orders on the hill called Olivet, the young men and women listening didn't know then that if they kept walking until they hit a point on this circular globe that, if they took one more step, they'd begin their journey home. If they had, they would have found a chain of islands in the South Pacific on the west side of what would later be defined as the International Date Line—quite literally, "coastlands"[24] in the sea where morning's first rays of sun hits their shores. They didn't realize some of the furthest soil from where they stood in the City of the Great King would later be founded as a city called "Christchurch."[25] That information would come to later generations in time. At that point, they knew they had a job to do: declare the King, the LORD God of Israel, to every people, nation, and language until—and so that—He would come again. Magnify the Name of the LORD. Sing this new song far and wide. Be walking witnesses of His Name, nature, and character throughout all the earth till Kingdom come.

Isaiah would later elaborate on the geographic trajectory of this new song, this new light that would dawn upon the Gentiles,[26] to color in the international intention of the Everlasting Covenant made with Abraham, Isaac, and Jacob. It would reach the very ends of the earth and begin to make its way back to the center—specifically reaching the Arab world as it filled in the gaps of Gospel-poverty before reaching Jerusalem. Literally ages before Muhammad introduced

---

20 Isaiah 24:14–16; 42:10–16; Zechariah 12:10; 14:1–5; Matthew 23:39; Acts 1:6–8
21 Acts 3:21
22 See Psalm 48:2; Ezekiel 5:5; Matthew 5:35
23 Isaiah 9:6; "wonderful counselor" better translates to this.
24 Isaiah 24:14–16; 42:10
25 Christchurch, New Zealand is one of the furthest inhabited geographic locations from Jerusalem.
26 Isaiah 49:6; 60:3

the demonic doctrine of Islam to the Arab world, Isaiah audaciously declared that Saudi Arabia will bow the knee before Jerusalem does.[27] Muslims from Mecca to Jordan, just across the river from the Holy City, will confess the Lordship of Jesus—they will sing this "new song"—and magnify the Name of the LORD *before Jerusalem does*, because *when* Jerusalem does, Jesus will have His feet on the Mount of Olives again, right where He gave marching orders to the apostolic witness to begin with.[28]

Missions is not about anything more or less than the simple delivery of the beautiful message: Behold, God is great, and *we can know Him in Christ*. We can be reconciled to God in Christ. We can become what we're built to be— in, through, by, and for Jesus, because Jesus.[29] This message is the designated means of mercy, and therefore must be verbally declared and tangibly demonstrated. It is the privilege of the people of Jesus to represent Him where He is not known. We cannot consider missions, the frontier, or any ministry in the earth—from our inner cities, orphanages, or affluent suburban Starbucks Bible studies—as anything other than the magnification of the Name of the LORD. He is to be made known. He is to be declared. He is to be demonstrated. To be this kind of witness, to serve as prophetic and apostolic messengers, is the foundation of what it means to never bear His holy Name in vain.[30] To do this, we must know Him for who He is. For that knowledge, we must look to the highest and holiest revelation of the Holy One—we must look to the very "Messenger of the covenant."[31]

---

27 See Isaiah 42:11; Kedar is conventionally the Arabian peninsula.
28 Isaiah 24:14–16; 42:10–16; Zechariah 12:10; 14:1–5; Matthew 23:39; Acts 1:6–8
29 See Ephesians 1:18; Colossians 1:10,15–18
30 Ephesians 4:1; Colossians 1:10; 1 Thessalonians 2:12
31 Malachi 3:1

Section Three

The Face of Messiah

*"For God, who said,
'Let light shine out of darkness,' has shone in our hearts
to give the light of the knowledge of the glory of God
in the face of Jesus Christ."*

2 Corinthians 4:6

CHAPTER SIX

The Beautiful Son

"HE COVER THE FACE OF HIS THRONE, spreads His cloud over it,"[1] said the grieving man whose crippled body lay riddled with pain, his heavy heart ridiculed by his presumptuous and easily swayed companions. "No man has ever seen God,"[2] said the beloved, and the man blinded by glory would elaborate: "He dwells in unapproachable light."[3] Yet He knows what is in darkness, and in man;[4] light dwells with Him, and the Light of the World[5] would reveal "deep and secret things"[6] at just the right time[7] with an added clause: No one has seen the High and Lofty One—except His Son;[8] and if human eyes and hearts could catch a glimpse of the Son, they'd see past the edges of His ways, hear beyond the whispers of His words,[9] and behold what no man nor woman has since the "mighty disaster theologians call 'the Fall'"[10]—the Father.[11]

1   Job 26:9
2   John 1:18; 1 John 4:12
3   1 Timothy 6:16
4   John 2:25
5   John 1:1–4,9; 8:12; 9:5
6   Daniel 2:22
7   Galatians 4:4
8   Isaiah 57:15; John 6:46
9   Job 26:14
10   Tozer, A.W. (1961). *The Knowledge of the Holy*. New York: HarperCollins, 9.
11   John 14:9

The moment a shame-shattered man and woman heard the first mention of the coming Deliverer, this promised Seed,[12] Hebraic expectations wrapped themselves around the hope of a good King. He appears in the shadows of Moses' books, in the whispers of David's psalms, and emerges on the horizon of all prophetic texts. Revelation hit a songwriter in David's tent and tabernacle one day, and he could hardly write quickly enough: "My heart overflows with a good theme—this song is a song about the good King."[13] The first verse of the song describes a King overflowing with grace (John the beloved would use similar language)[14] and victorious in battle, ruling over every nation with a just and eternal throne. This is not the only time these themes and choices of verbiage appear in Scripture.[15]

Defining this Messianic hope is the Davidic dream; when the well-meaning king committed to building a house for God, he heard this in response: "David, if I were hungry, I wouldn't tell you. But I love your heart. Your hands are far too filthy from war to build My 'house,' but I'll appoint that task to your son, and I'll also give you a better One. That Seed I promised to Eve? He'll be born to your grandson."[16] Any appetite dead to apathy was quickly whetted; *the Seed was coming*. When He came, war would end.[17] The Kingdom of God would knit itself to a renewed and restored earth, this created order heard groaning since human hearts first gave affection to the lies of the accuser.[18] David began to sing of this Man; a later prophet began to massage His mysteries into written words for the nation to pore over.

Isaiah built his book around a narrative of the servant of the LORD, beginning with the nation of Israel, charged from her inception with stewarding the hopeful mysteries of redemption, yet was forced by truth to acknowledge Israel's insufficiency as a faithful and final witness of the nature and character of God. She could not purely serve while she so frequently and violently strove against Him (it is

---

12 Genesis 3:15
13 A paraphrase of Psalm 45:1
14 John 1:16
15 Genesis 49:10; Psalm 72:1–20; Isaiah 2:1–4; 9:6–7; Isaiah 24:23; Micah 4:1–5
16 See 2 Samuel 7:1–29
17 Psalm 46:8–10; 72:1–20; Isaiah 2:1–4; 9:6–7; Micah 4:1–5
18 See Genesis 3:1–8

worth remembering here that her story is very much our story;).[19] In the climax of his messages, the Father of glory thunders through the prophet to the nation elected and forged to bear His witness and name: *Behold My Servant!* It is too simplistic and deprecating to stare only at Israel's—and our—insufficiencies, for "the gifts and callings of God are irrevocable,"[20] and we are meant to serve our King and bear His message to the rest of the world; Israel bears this calling still. These assignments do not erode to our faithlessness; rather, our merciful Maker redirects our gaze from our own navels to the preeminent One: "Look at Me and you'll see everything you're meant to be."

When we see Him, we see the Father who adopts us at great cost in great kindness for great purposes to great ages.[21] We see the Servant willing to wash the feet of His enemy.[22] We see the pastor and teacher unwilling to make a public object lesson of someone exposed for vile infidelity.[23] We see the heir of all things unwilling to circumvent sovereign calendars for His own gain;[24] unwilling to exploit;[25] unwilling to steal;[26] unwilling to bow out of difficulty and pain;[27] unwilling to be bribed[28] or publicly lauded[29] but very willing to be mocked, scourged, and blamed for a myriad of wicked things He did not do.[30] It is in the sight of the One fully God yet fully Man, who lived our lives to die our deaths, we behold everything we were designed and destined to become; if we really want our "best life now," it is best to bow and bend our knee to the One who made our frames and knit purpose into the fibers of our souls.[31]

---

19 I published *Confronting Unbelief: Your Soul and the City of the Great King* in 2018 under FAI Publishing to develop this point further.
20 Romans 11:29
21 Ephesians 2:4–10
22 See John 13:1–26
23 John 8:2–11
24 Matthew 4:1–10
25 John 4:1–26; this is how Jesus treated vulnerable women.
26 See Matthew 22:21
27 See Matthew 26:53
28 See John 3:1–36; there's no way to know Nicodemus' intentions for certain, but it is not impossible he first approached Jesus at night to try to pull this rising, charismatic religious and cultural figure to be the boy for the "Pharisee team."
29 See Matthew 8:4; 16:20; Mark 7:36; 8:30; 9:9; Luke 5:14; 8:56
30 Isaiah 53:4–6; Romans 3:25–27; 2 Corinthians 5:21
31 2 Corinthians 3:18

Angels would gather in the skies the night He took His first breath, serving as the supporting cast for a brave young woman willing to let her Maker mold her life,[32] and her young husband willing to let his Maker ruin his reputation.[33] The entrance of this Son would move heavenly hosts, wise men of old, and humble men with thankless jobs to come and see, come and stare, come and sing.[34] The revelation of God in the flesh of a Middle Eastern Man meant the holy could be seen by eyes scarred with sin, and the invitation was given at last to sons of Adam and daughters of Eve: return to the garden and receive a new covering and a new nature, undeserved gifts from the One of whom we hum, begging for a glimpse and nearness: O come, let us adore Him.

Behold the Servant.[35]

Behold the Son.[36]

Behold the Lamb.[37]

---

[32] Luke 1:38
[33] Matthew 1:18–25
[34] See Matthew 2:1–12; Luke 2:1–20
[35] See Isaiah 42:1; 52:13; Zechariah 3:8; Matthew 12:18
[36] Matthew 3:17; 17:5
[37] John 1:29,36

CHAPTER SEVEN

THE LORD WILL PROVIDE HIMSELF

THE STORY OF A COVENANTAL FATHER LEADING his thirty-something year-old covenantal son up a hill in Jerusalem, bound by wood, to make a *holocaust*[1] of his child, did not originate in the New Testament.

It was first told in Genesis.

Paramount to the testimony of Scripture is perhaps its most bizarre recorded incident, even recently facing controversy.[2] The word of the LORD came to Abraham, who answered thus: "Here am I."[3] This obedient man who left Ur the moment he was told heard again a response with marching orders:

"Take your son—your *only* son, your *beloved* son—to a hill in Moriah I will show you." Take your elected son to an elected hill (one which Scripture would later identify as a very significant hill in Jerusalem),[4]

---

[1] See Strong's 5928; the word for 'burnt offering' in vv.7-8 is where we get the word "holocaust" from, referring to an offering fully devoured by fire on the altar.

[2] Piper, J. "Defending My Father's Wrath," (2006). Minneapolis:Desiring God. Accessed July 2018. https://www.desiringgod.org/articles/defending-my-fathers-wrath.

[3] Genesis 22:1

[4] Genesis 22:2; 2 Chronicles 3:1

this son in whose veins runs the blood of the everlasting covenant, *and make a holocaust of him there.*

Offer your only son on a hill in Jerusalem as a burnt offering.

So this father of the covenant walked with his son of the covenant for three days—three long days during which the son was dead in the heart of his father,[5] whose only hope was unwavering confidence in the God who would raise the dead to keep His promises[6]—with two men on either side joining them on the journey, carrying the wood for the offering.

The promised son made his way to Jerusalem on a donkey,[7] looked around and asked his father along the way: "We have the wood and the fire, but where is the lamb?"[8]

His father assured him: "The LORD will provide Himself a lamb."[9]

Once the father of this confidence in the God who raises the dead bound his elect son of covenantal promise on the altar and reached for the blade to drain his blood, heaven arrested his hand.

"Don't touch him. Don't hurt him."[10]

And heaven provided a ram.

Abraham's burden to be conformed into the image of the God he confessed made an object lesson of his son that day; Isaac serves us with a "type and shadow"[11] depiction of the beloved, only, elect Son of the covenant to come, in whose veins carried the atoning blood of the everlasting covenant.[12] Yet the insufficient provision that saved Isaac's life left his question hanging over generations of his and Jacob's children for centuries to come:

"But where is the lamb?"

How will we get free from sin?

---

5   See Genesis 22:4
6   Hebrews 11:17-19
7   Genesis 22:3; John 13:12-15
8   Genesis 22:7
9   Genesis 22:8; the grammar of the text is often modified in translations to read instead, "God will provide *for* Himself a lamb." It's not as accurate.
10 Genesis 22:11-12
11 Colossians 2:17; Hebrews 8:5; 10:1
12 See Hebrews 13:20

Much later, a revival would hit a religious community with a renewed fervor to walk according to the way of the LORD. Crowds crossed the country to find a man in the desert who would dunk their bodies below the waterline as a sign of repentance, turning from sin, and leaving their old lives behind in the water. On one day not otherwise unlike any other, a tradesman from the north travelled to find John the Baptist along the Jordan River. It mattered not that they were cousins and had likely spent holidays together growing up; on this day, John saw his relative with revelatory eyes and declared confidently, out loud, in public, that he knew the answer to the question hanging over Israel since that afternoon on Moriah: the LORD will provide Himself, a Lamb.

And He was standing in front of the nation on the muddy riverbed of the Jordan.

Did John shout? Did he shake and utter a whisper? How did the people around him respond? Did they freeze in their steps, some shivering as they dried off from their own baptisms? Did they remember Isaac the moment John saw more than a cousin in the Man standing before him?

Whatever it looked and felt and sounded like, it was an answer long awaited.

"Behold the Lamb, who takes away the sins of the world!"[13]

When He went underwater, another Voice declared aloud:

"This is My beloved Son!"[14]

Abraham's sons and daughters met a Man that day knowing only that He was:

A Lamb. The Lamb. A Son. A beloved Son.

Whispers of prophets and patriarchs must've thrust themselves up their throats from their hearts.[15]

Between the patriarch Abraham and the baptizing prophet John are pages and pages and pages of Torah and prophets, laws and songs, testifying of all God was doing and would do in days to come.

---

13   John 1:29
14   Matthew 3:17
15   Matthew 12:34; Luke 6:45

Embedded in the texts are whispers and shadows of a King coming, a Son promised, and a Judge victorious. They pointed to a Son of Man who "must suffer"[16] to "fulfill"[17] all the Scriptures had spoken of Him.[18]

Many must wonder, as we read the Genesis account of the foreshadowed atonement, what that experience was like for Isaac. Moses didn't include many details from him in the record, but the math puts him at the age of an able-bodied man in his thirties.[19] Abraham was nearly pushing daisies when he fathered Isaac—there's no way he could strong-arm his son onto the altar. Isaac laid down willingly in submission to his father's will and purposes. It is no wonder modern teachers are tripping over this passage to such dramatic degree to suppose it misguided child abuse.[20] It's not an exchange of human finitude—rather, it screams to us of eternity, of the Son purposed before "let there be light" destroyed the darkness, of the Lamb slain "before the foundation of the earth."[21] Of the God who gives all.[22] Of costly love. Calvary love.

The Son promised to Eve would be provided by the LORD, the good Lamb who is also the good Shepherd would lay His life on the altar by His own will and volition.[23] Abraham did not force Isaac's hand, and no one—not Pilate, not Judas, not the nation of Israel claiming responsibility for His blood[24]—forced Jesus'. The promised "Son of David, Son of Abraham"[25] knew what He was doing long before He wove more foreshadows into Law,[26] Gabriel informed Mary she'd soon conceive an immaculate mystery,[27] before He slept where sheep

---

16 Luke 9:22, emphasis added
17 See Matthew 5:18; 26:56
18 See Luke 24:25-27
19 The text and Jewish tradition places Isaac somewhere in the range of 30-37 years old at the time of this event.
20 Piper, John. "Defending My Father's Wrath," (2006). Minneapolis:Desiring God. Retrieved from https://www.desiringgod.org/articles/defending-my-fathers-wrath
21 Genesis 1:3; 1 Peter 1:20; Revelation 13:8
22 See Philippians 2:5-11
23 Isaiah 53:7; John 10:11, 17-18
24 Matthew 27:25
25 Matthew 1:1
26 See Exodus 29:18; Leviticus 6:1-30
27 Luke 1:31

would eat,[28] before the Bread of Life[29] dipped His last meal in a bowl to feed His traitor.[30]

A grateful father likely wept on Moriah, the day his son was spared, the day a lamb was promised but a ram was provided; on that hill, named then by a thankful patriarch: "The-Lord-Will-Provide,"[31] and known ever since that "in the Mount of the Lord it shall be provided."[32]

Indeed, the Lord would provide Himself a lamb, and He would do so on the hill of the Lord. The Son of God, Man, and glory would face both the torment of Gethsemane and the death of Golgotha for the name of His Father[33] and the "joy set before Him,"[34] patterning for all who would follow and confess His name what it meant to truly live alive in this "present evil age,"[35] and earning the right to overturn Adam's disobedient decision in Eden so many suns ago.

---

28 Luke 2:7
29 John 6:35
30 See John 13:26
31 Genesis 22:14
32 ibid.
33 John 17:1
34 Hebrews 12:2
35 Galatians 1:4

CHAPTER EIGHT

All Things

"*LET THEM HAVE DOMINION,*"[1] declared the Godhead. Innate in the heart of man is the urge to rule, to reign; this has been true since Adam first inhaled the breath of God,[2] when he was knit with an ordained capacity for his calling. It is precisely because mankind—male and female—were given this charge upon our creation that the "ruler of this world"[3] now has such destructive authority to exercise: it was given to him when we first bought the lie.[4] The only way out of the quandary we're in now is for someone trustworthy to usurp the usurper and inherit everything. If the first lord over life on earth[5] was insufficient, and the current one is wrought with wickedness, we can only hope triumph will come to a worthy torchbearer by the end of this age. If no one does, we're doomed to our kangaroo courts and power grabs until our bloodlust spills every vein dry. We need a Savior King to save us from ourselves.

Conveniently for all of us, that is exactly the testimony of Scripture.

---

1   Genesis 1:26
2   Genesis 2:7
3   See John 12:31; 14:30; 16:11
4   See Genesis 3:1-7
5   See Genesis 2:26

As the revelation of Eden's whispered hope[6] unfolded over time, tremendous dignity was given to a shepherd boy who inherited another man's crown. "You, David," said the LORD. "He'll come through you."[7] His son Solomon would become a glimpse of another Man born to gossip-fodder circumstances,[8] known to heaven as "Beloved,"[9] destined to build a dwelling place for the Almighty on very real, tangible, earthen soil.[10] And so David could sing of his Son as his "Lord,"[11] a Man destined to inherit all things. Destined to inherit Adam's original dominion. Destined to inherit authority over every other crown and king. Destined to inherit the cosmic "title deed."[12]

The prophets and psalmists erupted with color to fill in the long-treasured sketch of the Son who would crush the serpent's head.[13] He would end war and conflict,[14] poverty,[15] and bring all injustice to a consummate conclusion in the climactic "restoration of all things."[16] His throne would reign over all others; His crown would bear the weight of a global theocracy bringing all mankind into enlightened obedience to their Maker.[17] He is the elect Son reigning from the elect hill in the elect city of the elect nation;[18] none will move Him. Coastlands will await His word.[19] Lesser rulers will prioritize His order.[20] Every people group will "stream" to see Him and hear His voice.[21]

---

6   See Genesis 3:15
7   See 2 Samuel 7:12-16
8   Solomon's mother was Bathsheba (see 2 Samuel 11); controversy also surrounded Jesus' conception (see Matthew 1:18-25; John 8:19).
9   2 Samuel 12:25
10 2 Samuel 7:13
11 Psalm 110:1; Matthew 22:45; Luke 20:44
12 I borrow this term from Mike Bickle. See "Jesus Received as King by All Nations (Rev. 5:12)" at https://ihopkcorg-a.akamaihd.net/platform/IHOP/1021/71/20141010_Jesus_Received_as_King_by_All_Nations_Rev.5.12_TMHE05_study_notes.pdf
13 Genesis 3:15
14 Psalm 46:9; Isaiah 2:2-4; Micah 4:1-5
15 Psalm 72:2,12-14
16 Acts 3:21
17 Isaiah 9:1-7
18 Psalm 2:6-9; 110:2
19 Isaiah 51:5; 60:9
20 Psalm 72:10-11; Revelation 21:24
21 Jeremiah 31:12

If we're squirming as we read this, we are not without reason. This degree of power would corrupt even the purest among us; there is no way to exact justice and execute fair rule without having the literal mind of God, without being above the coy eyes and back rooms of timeless mobs and mafia. Do we know anyone who can be trusted with such a task? Both the short and long answers conclude succinctly: no.

No one greets adulthood with a clear record of consistent selfishness. We all threw tantrums as toddlers. We all wanted all the toys at one point or another and grieved when we couldn't have them. Something deep within us wanted—and wants—toys that don't belong to us.

This is why we can't be trusted with ruling the entire world.

When the apostle John saw heaven and the One sitting on the everlasting throne of righteousness and justice,[22] he caught a glimpse of something in His right hand: a scroll,[23] effectively the "title deed" bearing rights and responsibilities to rule and reign and restore all things. As he saw it, he heard an angel cry out: "Who can take this?" More specifically, "who is worthy to take the scroll and break its seals?"[24] John would have heard the question and felt his own insufficiencies, not unlike Isaiah's experience in the same room seeing the same One on the same throne: "Woe is me, for I am unclean, and I come from a people who are unclean."[25] The question posed to Isaiah rendered the same kind of answer John felt deep in his bones: there is a need, and the solution isn't me.

"Who can declare My word, Isaiah?"

"Not me—my lips are filthy, and everyone I know's lips are filthy. I don't know what to do."

The LORD of righteousness had to make Isaiah clean to get the job done.

The cross of Christ was the legal transfer to remove Isaiah's filth and impute to him something qualifying, something beautiful.[26]

"Who can be trusted, John?"

---

22   Psalm 89:14; 97:2
23   Revelation 5:1
24   Revelation 5:2
25   Isaiah 6:5
26   See 2 Corinthians 5:21

The apostle wept. He knew it wasn't him. And he knew it wasn't any of his buddies.

Our best revelations of Jesus are found in the dirt of our own disappointments, when we're willing to lower our egos and face our own insufficiencies.

"I saw a Lamb standing, as though it had been slain...."[27]

The Man John once watched die, standing "nearby" alongside His grieving mother,[28] was alive and willing and qualified—because He was the Lamb, because He had everything and forfeit it all on behalf of His enemies, because He had prioritized His Father's glory under greatest duress.[29]

Turns out there's one toddler who survived childhood without becoming fertile soil to seeds of selfishness.

His name is Jesus.

It took God to conquer the flesh, and God to reconcile the fallen to the Holy. It is God and God alone who can be trusted to rule and reign and restore all things—and this was always the point. This age was always meant to exalt, elevate, and exonerate the Name of the Most High through unexpected means using unlikely people and unconventional things. Jesus could have pulled a Revelation 19 the first time He came, but He didn't. He also could've said no to the Place of the Skull before He laid the foundation of the world, but He said yes to this beautiful and precious dream long before light broke darkness for the first time. Paul was not out of line to suggest—rather declare—Jesus is destined to be "preeminent in all things."[30] All things. *All*.

"For in Him all the fullness of God was pleased to dwell, and through Him to reconcile to Himself all things, whether on earth or in heaven, making peace by the blood of His cross...to present you holy and blameless before Him."[31] "The Kingdom of Heaven is like a Father preparing a wedding for His Son."[32] Here is our lifeline, where we

---

27 Revelation 5:6
28 John 19:26
29 See Matthew 26:39; John 17:1-6
30 Colossians 1:18
31 Colossians 1:19-20,22, emphasis added
32 Matthew 22:2

find ourselves in this extravagant story. What is the point of life? To be found in Him. What is the essence of life? To know Him. Why the cross? To reveal Him. Why Jerusalem? To host Him. Why this age? To prepare us.

The Son destined to inherit Adam's original dominion, destined to inherit authority over every other crown and king, destined to inherit the cosmic "title deed" and rule and reign and restore all things is also destined as the second Adam to rule alongside the second Eve, the bride and Body of Jesus.

Section Four

Like a Bridegroom

*"In them He has set a tent for the sun, which comes out like a bridegroom leaving his chamber,
and, like a strong man, runs its course with joy.
Its rising is from the end of the heavens,
and its circuit to the end of them, and there is nothing hidden from its heat."*

Psalm 19:5

CHAPTER NINE

GRACE PERSONIFIED, THE WORD INCARNATE

ONE OF THE CAUSES AND EFFECTS TO THIS WONDROUS "BENEFIT"[1] we know as salvation is the "praise of the glory of His grace."[2] Grace is the engine, one of the means behind our salvation, and our praise of it is but one end.

Grace is recklessly extravagant favor, a gift no one could earn or deserve. It's what met the cheating baby of the family on the road outside of town before the neighbors could lynch him for his indiscretions.[3] It's what pushed Hosea out the door again and again and again. It's what brought Gomer home time after time after time. It's what met David on the backhills of Bethlehem, the backside of Ziklag, and the tail end of his days. It is what moved heaven to make earth, keep earth, and commit to preserve and restore her forever. It is what keeps breath in our lungs after blasphemy and insists on washing us after we've gone to bed in the mud for the umpteenth time. It is what apprehends a traitor before the noose falls around his neck; what adopts and transforms a child of wrath into a child of God

---

1   See Psalm 103:1-5
2   Ephesians 1:6
3   See Luke 15:11-32; Keller, Tim. *The Prodigal God: Recovering the heart of the Christian faith*, (2008). [Kindle DX version].

before the evil one claims her forever. Grace imparts the faith through which we're saved before we think or realize our need to ask for it. It is what examines our worthless merits and trades our bankruptcy for the bank account of our Father in heaven. Words will fail to explain grace forever, and so forever will be filled with our songs delighting in it, and in Him who authored this mighty, courageous thing that transformed us into children of the Most High, beloved of Jesus.

Grace is what made Paul a messenger, what taught him how to pour cement for the more excellent house.[4] It is what pulled his audiences and earliest disciples out of the otherwise impenetrable darkness of the god of this world.[5] The stars which led wise men to a manger and hosted the choirs of heaven to tell shepherds of the newborn King are the same that shone to sing of something like a second sun, a second light let come.

As dawn first began to break over the cosmos and created order, the Word of the Maker of Heaven and Earth swelled and echoed into galaxies and orbits, supernovas and sunshine. Oceans were organized. Continents were given place and shorelines upon which tidal patterns could crash and go no further.[6] Trees were planted, stars ordained, and animals fashioned so they could later be paraded and named.

The psalmist would later reflect on Genesis' account of earth's earliest days, digging out attributes and actions not immediately detailed in Moses' account in the Torah. David began the nineteenth psalm highlighting ongoing purpose and witness within created order, beginning with everything beyond the boundaries of our small planet circling its limited axis.

> *"The heavens declare the glory of God, and the sky above [the same expanse mentioned in Genesis 1:6-8] proclaims His handiwork."*

The skies shout to us every day: "Look at what He made!" This fact would cause David to stare at the stars in awe, and wonder why God

---

[4] See Psalm 127:1; 1 Corinthians 1:1; 2:3; 2 Corinthians 5:1; Ephesians 3:7-8; 4:7; Galatians 1:15-16
[5] See 2 Corinthians 4:4
[6] See Job 38:11

bothered to make mankind at all.[7] "Day after day pours out speech, and night to night reveals knowledge." *Reveals knowledge.* So much was placed for us to see, observe, and learn from- to perceive, understand, and know the nature and character of the One who put it all there. Paul would later cite the cosmos as a case against pagans, guilty before God despite never having been given the luxury of the Law as the Hebrews had been. "His invisible attributes, namely, His eternal power and divine nature, have been clearly perceived, ever since the creation of the world, in the things that have been made. So they are without excuse."[8] Everything within and beyond the Milky Way has testified to His name, nature, and character since before man was formed in Eden. "There is no speech, nor are there words, whose voice is not heard. Their voice goes out to all the earth, and their words to the end of the world."

Prophets would elaborate on David's sung revelation, the appointed destiny of the Word of the LORD to reach every corner of the world. Jesus Himself would reiterate it and command our participation.[9] Everything beyond our galaxy testifies to His glory, their voices harmonizing with the choirs of heaven, and it is thus appallingly unjust and inappropriate that corners and crevices of this singular planet either don't know His name or blaspheme the one they've heard. Indeed, creation groans under the weight of Eden's curses and would itself cry out to praise Him if we—those made in His image—failed to do our part.[10]

Psalm 19 isn't a singular case of Scripture. In the years of the prophets and patriarchs, the LORD often pointed to His heavenly handiwork as a witness of His covenantal purposes. He once said through Jeremiah, "When the sun and stars fall out of the sky, I've abandoned Israel," (essentially, when hell freezes over).[11] Isaiah looked to a day when the glory of the LORD was so tangibly present on earth that it shamed the moon and sun.[12] Until then, the grandeur of the cosmos continues to demonstrate His power, testify His name to the Gospel-poor, affirm

---

7   See Psalm 8:3-4
8   Romans 1:20
9   See Matthew 24:14; 28:18-20; Acts 1:8
10 See Romans 8:19-22; Luke 19:40; Genesis 1:26-27
11 Jeremiah 31:36
12 Isaiah 24:23

His covenant, challenge man's conscience, and provide a literal, daily portrait of the light that breaks into the black of night to dispel darkness so mankind may walk in light.

In these heavenly choruses "He has set a tent for the sun, which comes out like a bridegroom leaving his chamber, and, like a strong man, runs its course with joy." Paul, the pioneer architect of the better house, once explained the better way as the kind of covenantal commitment that "endures all things,"[13] never-ending. Never giving up. "Endure" in the thirteenth chapter of his first letter to the Corinthians—who were up to their eyeballs in sin and corporate compromise—means to bravely bear, to face the firefight without thought of retreat.[14] David woke up on Bethlehem's backhills with his father's sheep, and learned something about God in the sun, which rose and warmed him like twenty-four-hour clockwork: *He's like a husband.* He's like a radiant man covenantally committed to his bride, who never jumps ship, never bails on His word. Never quits the race before He hits the finish line. *He started something here, and He's going to finish it.* "Its rising is from the end of the heavens, and its circuit to the end of them, and there is nothing hidden from its heat." Nothing escapes His gaze.[15] No one is excluded from the baseline of common grace.[16]

He is the Master Craftsman; He builds nothing without purpose. Everything fashioned by His hand is meant to depict something, but only one thing in the whole of His "good" creation was made in His image.[17] Walking mirrors were formed from dust, rib, and blood to further display His glory—and, uniquely, the greatness of the glory of His grace.

When the Lord made mankind, male and female both, He planted a Garden to put us in. It's the first holy Garden we see in creation.

It won't be the last.

---

13 1 Corinthians 12:31b, 13:7-8
14 "Hypomenō," Strong's G5278
15 2 Chronicles 16:9; Proverbs 15:3
16 Matthew 5:45
17 Genesis 1:10,12,18,21,25,31

CHAPTER TEN

A TYPE OF HIM WHO WAS TO COME

WITH FOUR FINITE WORDS, the One who dwells in unapproachable light allowed light to shine,[1] to spread over an infant creation and carry His word in its beams. Everything in heaven and on earth is made to proclaim His attributes and matchless glory. In Him and through Him all things consist, and for Him all things exist.[2] He spoke and grace like words poured out and made stuff[3] that in turn speaks to sing the praise of the One who is truth.[4] There was an age of honesty before deceit first leaked, and Genesis 1 describes it to us. No lie had yet been heard, no non-truth yet reverberated through chambers of neither the universe nor the human ear. There was a day something other than truth was uttered, and it was no accident. Everything has a purpose under heaven,[5] and we are no exception. It may in fact be truer to say mankind serves an exceptional purpose under heaven.

---

1   See 1 Timothy 6:16
2   See Colossians 1:16-17
3   See Psalm 45:2
4   See John 14:6
5   Ecclesiastes 3:1

Consider this age He very deliberately purposed, that this play written to declare everything about Him would be set on a very particular stage, and it would feature very peculiar creatures and characters in starring roles. Of all the birds of the air, fish of the sea, trees of the forest, or creatures with beating hearts, only one was made to mimic and mirror the glorious God who spoke everything into existence.

Spoke, that is, until He got His holy hands dirty.

One of the "psalms of ascent," traditionally sung as worshippers made their way to the top of Zion's hill to worship the LORD of Hosts, asks who could rival God in His matchless humility, crediting how low He must stoop to peer upon "the things that are in heaven and on the earth."[6] Everything is petty compared to Him. Everything and everyone is beneath Him. He peers anyway. Time and Scripture would reveal breathtaking mysteries to His limitless lack of ego, but mere creation is sufficient to speak of for now.

Bending down in unfathomable, immeasurable condescension—more than need be required to tell the stars to shine—the Holy and humble Maker of Heaven and Earth and all that is within it pushed His hand into clay and scooped up red earth and a handful of dust. It is worth pointing out here to wonder; why handle something so literally and figuratively beneath Him? What could He have in mind for such humble, lowly material? Imagine, now, the host of heaven watching, staring, waiting with bated breath to see what He intended to do. Here began the earliest glimpses of a long and complicated story, full of every epic necessity; romance, betrayal, monarchy, victory. An elderly apostle would write, much later down the track of human history, to tell us of heaven's angels but peer into and wonder at this mystery.[7]

If He had it in His holy mind to insert a walking mirror upon the earth, He had options to work with. He chose dirt.[8] Dirt. He chose the least dignified means available to fashion it into His likeness and set it on this grand stage designed to display His unrivaled grandeur. After considering every artistic option on the table, His matchless mind concluded that the best means to provide created order with a

---

6   See Psalm 113:6
7   See 1 Peter 1:12
8   See Genesis 2:7

living, breathing display of who He is and what He's like on Earth, is to use the stuff that gets scraped off shoes before anybody crosses the threshold of a door."

Dirt.

It would be a bit insulting if it weren't for the holy dignity of His incredible humility. He stoops and condescends; thus His image-bearers would find their first form in the lowest means available. Dust assembled and lungs filled with the holiest means, man opened his eyes immediately and was ever sustained by the breath of God. This first man, the first male of mankind, was the first to enter into the mandate given just after the Holy determined to "let Us"[9] make walking mirrors and install them on the walls of the world. Both man and woman were made to succeed, build families, cultivate the earth and live as the utmost authority over it, as both stewards and monarchs.

Every mention of dominion in the first two chapters of the Scriptures refers to the kind of rule and reign over land and territory reserved for what we understand to be kings and queens. The explosive events in the first chapter of Genesis led to a creation designed specifically to declare the works and knowledge of the One who made it, and an entire planet was handed over to these muddy creatures made to look a bit like Him. Mankind, in our first breaths and motions, lived as a king and queen over earthen territory given to us by Him who ordained the circle of the world, and filled it with everything living and seen. It was a blank and beautiful slate, and it was ours. This gift whispered what we would later hear from the Father of glory, "You've always been with Me, and all I have is yours."[10]

Genesis' first passages build the basis for our rhythmic work weeks, with days of labor, errands, and obligation peppered with a regular day of rest. Modern science and psychology attest to physiological, emotional, relational, and cognitive benefits to this kind of Sabbath cycle[11] which has origin in "the history of the heavens and the earth when they were created, in the day that the LORD God made the

---

9   Genesis 1:26
10   Luke 15:31
11   Dein, S. & Loewenthal, K.M. J Relig Health (2013) 52: 1382. https://doi.org/10.1007/s10943-013-9757-3.
     Smith-Gabaj, H. & Ludwig, F. (2011) Observing the Jewish Sabbath: A Meaningful Restorative Ritual for Modern Times, Journal of Occupational Science, 18:4, 347-355, DOI: 10.1080/14427591.2011.595891.

earth and the heavens."[12] Imagine inheriting limitless possibilities in work you deeply, intrinsically enjoyed, with the blessing of your Father serving as the wind in your sails. Money wasn't an object, and success was guaranteed. "Work. Rest. Enjoy." Those made in the Image of the Maker would make, craft, and thrive. Just as the solar system, both oceans and African wildlife exist to declare something about the nature and character of God- and so do we. Mankind, both men and women, are very deliberately designed and very specifically assigned to great work and glorious tasks. We are, primarily, written and wired to play our part in the "Greatest Story Ever Told."

Under these premises and this canopy of Edenic trees, this early garden became the conduit of communion between mankind and our Maker. This is before deception, betrayal, violations, treason, infidelity, and before fig leaves. Shame knew no place in Eden. We did not recoil when the Holy One entered and called our name. Tasks were initiated, goals completed. Work was satisfying, yet not ultimate. More than anything, a friendship was forged between the Image and His bearer. Conversations filled the corridors. Dialogue and dreams were exchanged. Innocence saturated the air. Safety undergirded every emotion. We don't know how much time passed, how many suns rose and set, with happy Paradise as all mankind had ever known. Our first father and mother, the patriarch and matriarch of mankind, knew Earth before the ravages of war, the terror of crime, the fracture of family units, or the poison of ill-sought relief. They did, however, watch it make the transition, so perhaps there is less to envy.

A fracture did come, a fault line wanting to rip this holy sanctuary to shreds. War crept into the wilderness of Eden on the heels of treason. Shame encased our frames, coaxed us to flee into hedges and cover ourselves in fig leaves (which, incidentally, caused rashes and burning sensations).[13] Torment began to haunt our hearts, bodies and minds. We became victims of our own indiscretions. Mankind's treason in the Garden opened the floodgates to a kind of all-encompassing poverty we could not have fathomed, yet have drowned in such ever since. It opened a corridor of suffering we would have to walk down till Kingdom come.

---

12   Genesis 2:4

13   Canadian First Aid Courses. (2015). Fig allergy rash. Retrieved from http://canadian-firstaidcourses.ca/fig-allergy-rash/ 22 January 2017.

It is not all for naught; Paul levels suffering with hope, with holy logic confounding our post-Enlightenment, post-modern Western worldviews.[14] According with the Jew entrusted with the task of bringing the Gospel to pagan Gentiles, we've been drinking from the well of sin and shame since God first wondered aloud why we hid from Him, and suffering is a conduit of a better spring.[15] It embeds and implants endurance within us—the "I'm not going anywhere" kind of commitment—that forges character and conviction deep within who we are. Just as fire burns away dust and chaff to bring forth pure gold,[16] so suffering forges us. We generally think of it simply as a consequence of sin (and it is), but Jesus is the "lamb slain from before the foundations of the earth,"[17] which means suffering isn't an accident or by-product of this age. Rather, it is part and parcel to it, and we have been given access to gain gold by it. There are hills to mine, saints. Let us not scorn their caverns and fires.

Suffering is the soil and seedbed of hope, a bittersweet tenet of this age through which we "believe without seeing."[18] It echoes in our cries for the Father we've been too far from for far too long, and will not go unanswered.[19] This is His holy Word's infallible promise to us: We will never be embarrassed for hanging our hopes on the One who hung on wood cursed to meet the conditions of mankind's judicial sentencing.[20] To everything there is a purpose under heaven; to everything, a time and a season. This "present evil age" will serve us purged and precious memories for all eternity to come when we meet the Comforter.[21]

Christ made this backwards logic possible and powerful through His work on the cross of Golgotha. The Incarnate Word became the form of His form, a global race wrought with decay and bound to besetting sin. The fullness of God dwelt on earth in bodily form,[22] lived a life we couldn't live and died a death we were supposed to die, and in so

---

14 See Romans 5:1-5
15 See Galatians 2:7; John 4:10-15
16 See Psalm 12:6 Proverbs 27:21; 1 Peter 1:7; Revelation 3:18
17 Revelation 13:8
18 John 20:29
19 Romans 8:15; Galatians 4:6
20 Deuteronomy 21:23; Galatians 3:13
21 Galatians 1:4; see John 14:16; 2 Corinthians 1:3-7
22 See John 1:14; Philippians 2:5-11; Colossians 1:19

doing saved our lives, souls and minds from the clutch of the evil one who led us to believe our earliest lies about the character of our holy Father in heaven. We can but speculate what it would be like to be God, take on the form of God to ransom traitors off of Death Row, die the most excruciating death, and feel forsaken by God.[23] Not long after Christ's death, resurrection, and ascension, one man wrote the letter to the Hebrews and put it this way: the Son of God "learnt obedience by the things He suffered," having tasted death "by the grace of God," authoring salvation for all who call on His name.[24] For all this, is was appropriate that He endured suffering. We suffer, He suffered. It is an incredible thing.

Our suffering, then, is traced back to Adam and Eve's treason in the Garden. In Romans 5,[25] Paul specifically pins responsibility for our ongoing death and deterioration on Adam's solitary act of disobedience. His treason, conviction of guilt, and corresponding sentencing to capital punishment cursed us all to enter our lives in this age with the same. The apostle's letter to the Romans compares Adam's costly, disobedient blunder with Christ's selfless and sacrificial obedience—yet he does not instruct us to see and learn from the disparity altogether. He calls that first man formed in Eden's early rays a "type of Him who was to come."[26]

It's easy to read Romans 5 and think to yourself, "Paul—did you miss 'Opposite Day' at school? You *just* explained how those two men are very, very different. One man sinned. The other Man served. Consider the consequences! Look at what Christ achieved—one man died and we all died with him. The other Man died so we could all live again. *Different*." I believe this is where the aged apostle would lean in to us over the table, smile slight, and say, "Different, but not in so many ways." We are so familiar with the story of Adam and Eve, it is commonly (and erroneously) considered folklore—even within the Church, and even amongst many of us who intellectually assent to Genesis 1-3 being a real and true historical account. We're so distanced and divorced from our grandparents that we can't relate to them anymore, yet we're so familiar with their Fall we can't see the

---

23 See Matthew 27:46
24 Hebrews 2:9-10; 5:8
25 See Romans 5:6-20
26 Romans 5:14

proverbial forest for the trees. There is something holy here revealed in the fifth chapter of Romans, and it demands we take our time and prayerfully examine what holy mystery the apostle pointed us to. Adam was a prototype of the coming Messiah, even in light of the fact that his disobedience was nothing like Jesus' obedience, and his traitor's curse obligingly passed to generations was nothing like Jesus' free gift of reconciliation to God all at once. That should confound us and cause us to revisit and retrace our early Edenic sun with wonder in our hearts.

CHAPTER ELEVEN

A Suitable Companion

IN MANKIND, WE SEE NOT ONLY GLIMPSES of the Holy personality and nature, but also a cosmic witness of His revelation at large. Long after Eden, Paul would submit that the whole purpose of this age's revelation of God would be to display His nuanced, dynamic, and colorful wisdom through His people to the powers and principalities in the heavens.[1] The universe is a stage, and He is the star. He could have scripted it any number of ways, yet this is the way He chose in this age—through the lives and mirrors of mankind. He deliberately didn't make a male human and stop there. He deliberately didn't leave Adam alone. He deliberately decided the man needed "a suitable companion,"[2] He deliberately made a woman as well. Femaleness and femininity were yet required to properly reflect the nature and knowledge of God within creation, and complement the image of God reflected in masculinity already provided by Adam. Then the LORD stopped creating things. *Then* it was all "very good."[3]

We aren't told how long Adam spent naming animals, but we're told he named them all. More accurately, we're told the LORD observed a lack in the man's life ("It isn't good for him to be alone; I'm going to

---

[1] See Ephesians 3:8-13
[2] See Genesis 2:18
[3] Genesis 1:31

make him a comparable helper")[4] and *then* suddenly he is tasked with naming all the animals. Meaning this: the man wasn't aware of any lack. The fact that he was the singular example of his kind had not yet occurred to him, or it did and he didn't care. The LORD was sufficient for Adam. Edenic man experienced no lack. His nights were plagued by exactly no insecurities. He was not lonely. He was only alone, and that is a very different thing. Yet we see something emerge in Adam meant to depict something in the heart of God: desire for a suitable companion.

Desire is a recurring theme throughout Scripture, but we don't need to read about it in a book to know it embeds everything we think, say, and do like an unmanageable undercurrent beneath our psyche, a riptide we so often drown in. Freud, Jung, and Pavlov would all explore volumes' worth of material, yet their contributions to understanding psychology were weighed and found wanting. Desire is the force that overflowed "let there be…" and "let Us make…" from the heart of God, spilling forth from the well which bends the mouth to speak.[5] Desire is what produced mankind, and desire is what made the world prepare for a woman's introduction.

Adam's Maker begins to introduce the man to every other living creature upon the earth, and bestows upon him the dignity of naming them all (a privilege inherent with the rulership and authority given to him). In all likelihood, Adam can count just fine and begins to realize that every other living creature exists in multiples. More than one elephant roamed around the seedbed of creation. More than one lizard, more than one bird, more than one fish. Lots of different kinds of whales swam the seas in pods and sang their own particular brand of songs. Eventually, the man would have realized every creature under heaven existed in more than one singular expression. Adam may not have been lonely, but he was alone, and now His Maker was fashioning a longing within him for a comparable companion. He was about to take a nap and wake up to the thing he never knew he needed, and creation's portrait of God's person, plan, and purposes would have every piece and character required to paint this multi-colored masterpiece.

---

4   Genesis 2:18
5   Genesis 1:3,26; Matthew 12:34; Luke 6:45

Opening his eyes to what I can only assume was blinding pain in his side, the man beheld a new creation, new creature he'd never seen and hadn't named. But he knew she was his, and he was hers. Libraries and letters are filled with poems and prose, but the first ever devised in the mind of man erupted in Eden's marriage ceremony: "Bone of my bone, flesh of my flesh..."[6] is more than endearing. For Adam and his wife, it was literal. He woke up missing a rib, rubbing a blood-stained scar in his side. She was not made from dirt. She was made from him. This made her altogether different from every other living thing, every other creature he had named, and anything his eyes had ever fallen upon in his life to that point. Mankind's decree for dominion was given to both genders in the heart and mind of God before He first touched dust to craft our eldest grandfather; Adam's responsibility, though, uniquely carried this woman carved out of his frame to live alongside and help him.

Interestingly, the "helper" here designed is the only recipient of the word `ezer, or "help meet," in Scripture aside from the LORD Himself.[7] This companionship was no insignificant or secondary role to fill. Before the writer of Genesis introduces us to this final creation, a pattern is displayed: the LORD worked a ton, and then made a companion for Himself in the form of His form, image of His likeness. Mankind was always decreed for two forms, yet male was fashioned first and subjected to the same pattern: work, cultivate, name things—and long for a suitable companion. Work and love were good and holy things before the Fall, and can be good and holy things again. We work because we look like the One who works. We love because we look like the One who is love.[8] Yet there is more to the story. Mankind is not a frivolity, nor an accidental growth out of a chemically-charged pond. The image and likeness of God was fashioned specifically for God, and no matter how much we may want to go about our business by ourselves, we will never be able to rid ourselves of the One we look like. We are His "suitable companion."

---

6   Genesis 2:23

7   'ezer, Strong's H5828. Speaking of women once (Genesis 2:18,20) and the LORD twelve times (Exodus 18:4; Deuteronomy 33:7,26,29; Psalm 20:2; 33:20; 89:19; 115:9-11; 121:1-2; 124:8; 146:5; Hosea 13:9); the word is also used three times to illustrate the futility of relying on anyone but the LORD (Isaiah 30:5; Ezekiel 12:14; Daniel 11:34).

8   1 John 4:19

This is why Paul's theology transcended the simple contrasts we learned in school on Opposite Day.

Eve did not lose her calling to her treason. The gifts and callings of God are irrevocable,[9] and Eve's Maker met our grandmother in the immediate wake of her most historically stupid and destructively selfish decision with gentle mercies. He covered her when she felt most exposed and most ashamed. Was she meant to rule and reign? Yes. Will she? Yes. Eve will, and we will, be a suitable companion to the One we're made from and for through all the ages to come—because of, and through faith in, the intercession of Jesus. And, through her testimony and God's incredible sovereignty over our history, we know so much more about Jesus than we would have if Eden never knew the whispers of deceit, never knew the tremors of treason. We know the God who intervenes—He is the Lamb who leads Himself to the slaughter. The Spirit who intercedes when we're eyeing up another piece of forbidden fruit.

Humanity is a collision of broken mirrors, a kaleidoscope of children who look like their grandparents and humans who look like the God we've spent an age forsaking. Yet just as no child can fully excommunicate themselves from their gene pool and genealogy, no man nor woman can fully escape the blazing heart of the One who formed and fashioned them in their mother's womb. We are His mirror, His likeness; we are the form of His form, and we couldn't change ourselves if we tried (though we do try). The Fall of mankind, our fracture from safe and undefiled companionship and communion with our Maker, was not as though we fell into a hole. As with all sin and treason, it came after a sequence sliding us down a muddy hill with almost nothing to grab a hold of on the way down. We are, to be sure, without excuse,[10] but our exile from Eden is not the consequence of an algebra equation, and cannot be easily or simply explained. Hearts, desires, dreams, and deceit all wove the noose with which we hung ourselves. It was a very human exchange, and soberly so; we are not unfamiliar with our own complexities. We dance with the same demons every day. If all Adam was was a love-drunk fraud, he wasn't the type of Him who was to come Paul so confidently declared him to be. There is always more to the story.

---

9   Romans 11:29

10   See Romans 1:20

CHAPTER TWELVE

DECEIT AND EDENIC GRAVEDIGGING

JESUS' SACRIFICIAL SUFFERING IN OUR STEAD was in His mind and heart before we fell. It is a strategy He dreamt up long before we rebelled.[1] The Cross was always His intention; He'd well embedded its jurisdiction within the very Law of Moses.[2] Eden's collapse came as no surprise to the sovereign Son of Man. The snake didn't sneak into the Garden past the omniscient sight of the One with blazing eyes.[3] The tree bearing fruit that would bring this infant Paradise to an early death didn't grow on its own accord. What we have to come to terms with is a bitter providence: Jesus let that snake within Eden's borders. Jesus put that tree there. He let its seed grow roots and stretch into branches upon which would hang a seductively appealing fruit. He did that. More than anything, He wasn't around to shoo the snake off or tell Eve again not to touch the wrong tree. Tangible absence was His deliberate decision.

Tozer's assertion that what we believe about God is the most important thing about us[4] is not only true regarding the macro-philosophies

---

1   Romans 8:29; Ephesians 1:4; 3:9-11; 1 Peter 1:19-20; Revelation 13:8
2   See Galatians 3:13-14 (cf. Deuteronomy 21:23)
3   See Revelation 1:14
4   Tozer, A.W. *The Knowledge of the Holy*, (1961). New York: HarperCollins. p. 1.

and worldviews shaping and governing our lives. Our idea of God, right or wrong, bears down upon our consciences and thought lives and conversations unlike any other concept we could ever entertain, and it is purest when we're left to our own devices. My friend calls this our "pillowtop theology," what we believe when no one else is around to distract us, when there are no songs or services to influence us, when there are no platforms or pulpits to influence us; at the end of the day, when we put our heads on our pillows, we believe what we really believe about ourselves, our lives, and our Maker. Insomnia, anxieties, and dreams each betray what we believe to be true, for good or ill. If, at our core, we believe Jesus to be something like a mild-mannered hippie who just wants to hug everybody, Eden's limitations will offend us. Golgotha will disgust us, and His return to the Mount of Olives will repulse us. If we believe Him to be supreme, sovereign, wise, and kind no matter what He decides (because He has proven Himself to be faithful and unwavering), we will feel much safer swimming through deeper themes in the ocean that is the knowledge of God.

The moment truth ceased to be the only spoken thing, it was targeted at the only woman on the earth. From "let there be light" until the serpent approached her in the Garden, no tongue had ever uttered deceit. No ear had ever entertained perversion. No mind had ever gotten drunk on delusion. This bliss came to a subtle halt with four seductively strung words: "Did God really say?" Truth and the integrity of the Word of the LORD came under joint attack because they are one and the same; He was the first object of assault, and she was the strategically-targeted victim. All of humanity would be conceived in her womb. Every son and daughter to come would trace their roots back to her motherhood. Mankind hinged on this matriarch, and here it was all subject to abortion.

Satan did not sneak into this Garden. The tree of the knowledge of good and evil didn't spring up on its own. Job wasn't put to the test without God's permission; his trials were, in fact, the LORD's idea.[5] He instigated Job's troubles. Nothing in Scripture makes the case for a Sovereign God who didn't know Paradise was under assault, who doesn't direct the path of even lying spirits.[6] This has been about

---

5   See Job 1:6-12
6   2 Chronicles 18:18-22; 1 Kings 22:13-23

the integrity of His Word from the very beginning, and now it was under fire. Genesis 3 makes it clear that mankind was never built with the intestinal fortitude to withstand temptation and resist sin and the serpent's schemes. We were always designed to need the Helper. We were all made for lifetimes of "come to Jesus" moments. Our grandmother faced the first one. She took knowledge apart from the omniscient One instead. We've been born into delusion ever since.

Deceit danced its way through the Word of the LORD to pervert her knowledge of the LORD and evaporate her fear of the LORD, succeeding on every count. Ultimately, the lie achieved making God out to be a liar. This is the singularly most blasphemous idea—that He who is "the Truth"[7] has in Him even a shred of deceit. Nevertheless, convinced that the Father from whom all good things have their origin[8] had misled and withheld from her, she violated the only law binding her will and abandoned obedience to become a transgressor. The delusion of the lie led humanity from deception to treachery, and in reaching out for a violation of covenantal security, she betrayed both her Maker and her husband—in that order. Extending to offer it to her other half was a merciless extension of infidelity, an invitation to die with her.

He took it. There's no getting around the disastrous fire of treason started with this proverbial match; its burn has scarred the skin of every man and woman since this first man and woman struck it against their insubordination and infidelity. He knowingly disobeyed express instructions, willfully defied boundaries drawn around his safety, and drunkenly violated his pure and open-handed communion with the Holy. When all was said and done, when fig leaves were sewn into cloaks, when eyes once full of light began to flicker, and shame began to infect the consciences of once-innocents, traitors were summoned by their judicial and compassionate Maker: "What have you done?"[9]

Nobody lied. Eve and Adam both came clean. It is too easy to read the dialogue in Genesis 3 and dismiss it off as cowardly blame-shifting. The LORD's first question to the man was "Where are you?" He didn't accuse, though He was fully aware of what happened. He

---

7   John 14:6
8   See Genesis 3:13a
9   See Genesis 3:13a

didn't even ask "Why are you hiding?" but Adam answered as though He had. It is as if Adam felt foreign, and didn't know how to process what just happened to him, what he just did. "I heard You, and I was afraid"—he'd never had need to feel afraid before—"because I was naked"—this is only news to him, really—"and I hid myself."[10]

Adam's words mark the first time in human history we hid from God simply because of what we knew ourselves to be. For the first time, he felt insecure and insufficient before the LORD not necessarily because of who he was, but what he was. Naked—which he had been for some time, but what changed for Adam that day was his sense of shame. Eden exposed mankind for what we are without the covering of the LORD, a lesson to be remembered until we are fully and finally cloaked in His righteousness.[11] The first and most tangible symptom of injustice was shame then and is shame now. We can cope with a calloused conscience if we choose to, but nothing haunts the human heart like the permeating cloak of shame.

Imagine your child does something incredibly stupid while you're out of the room. Say they stuck their hand on a red-hot stove top, despite the fact that you've told them not to a thousand times and warned them all you could, but nobody really understands what it means to get burned when they're three years old. You walk back into the kitchen and they're hiding in the cupboard with the pots and pans. They're making a ruckus. You know exactly where they are, but you ask them anyway. They sheepishly reply from inside the cupboard and tell you that they ducked in with the pots and pans the moment they heard you because they were scared, because they were infantile, so they hid. You know full well their hand is burnt and blistering and needs immediate medical attention, but that's not what the conversation is about anymore. "Who told you you're a kid with an under-developed frontal lobe?" When did that become a bad thing? Of *course* they're infantile and childish and made a super dipstick decision. They'll hit puberty and develop deeper cognitive capacities, and you know that. Of *course* Adam was uncovered. The LORD knew he was and wouldn't always be; it's always been in the heart of God to be our covering, to cloak us in His own righteousness. Why did the man suddenly have a guilt complex about something he couldn't control

---

10   Genesis 3:10
11   Romans 3:21-22; 10:4; 2 Corinthians 5:21; Revelation 3:5

and couldn't change? He digested a different knowledge. Replace the red-hot stove-top with watching Allied forces' film reels of liberating Dachau and Auschwitz. It was more than the man could handle. He was insufficient for that kind of knowledge. We are insufficient for that kind of knowledge.

Allegories and illustrations find their finite limitations quite quickly, as our toddler with a burnt-hand does. Notice, though, that the LORD didn't immediately retort or chastise Adam with any kind of, "Well, yeah, you are, you nitwit. You disobeyed Me, didn't you?" He has always been a Father, and His son was feeling the sting of shame. No good parent *enjoys* it when their kid (or teenager, or grown adult) feels like an idiot, even in deserving circumstances. No; His tone was soaked in compassionate grace. "Who told you you were naked? Did you seek wisdom and knowledge apart from life in Me?"[12]

This is the point in reading the narrative that gets taught and talked about like everybody was just pointing fingers and placing blame, like mankind and Satan got caught in a preschool brawl and no one wanted to take responsibility for it. The thing is, neither the man nor the woman lied about their involvement. Nobody tried to cover their tracks. Everybody said exactly what happened how it happened. The LORD asked the man not where he got the information he was naked, but by whom he had been informed, and whether or not he ingested what he wasn't supposed to. Adam said, yes; "she gave it to me, and I ate it." He didn't claim Eve had shoved it down his throat. He confessed: "She gave it to me, and I ate it." So the LORD turned to her: "What is this you've done?"

Peer into this.

Mankind was made in two forms; for and from each other. She was made from this man to share life with this man. Together, they were given the highest dignity (to bear the image of God) and privilege (to rule over the creation of God). They were literally one flesh forming two bodies, and she violated the covenant. She defected. She broke rank and toyed with the enemy's grenade. She pulled the pin. It would have been just as vile if Adam had done the same, and Scripture holds him to account for his own part, but she didn't rebuke the snake. She bought his lie. Her purchase didn't only have consequences on her

---

12 See Genesis 3:11

and her own life. As with most sin, it affected everyone closest to her as well. The grenade had an explosive radius, and now her husband bled with her.

It was true for her to say, "The snake deceived me, and I ate." Satan didn't simply lie to her. He *convinced* her of the lie. We could rail on her for being so gullible, for lacking any discernment to refute something that is (to us) so brazenly untrue. But we read Genesis 3 with the luxury of retrospect—and the rest of Scripture. She had never heard a lie before. Delusion was *foreign* to her. She was young, a little dumb, and altogether naive. The snake didn't feed her a whole load of bull; all of his schemes are grounded in truth, with just enough perversion to pull us off the narrow way.

The LORD didn't bother to ask the enemy what he did or why he did it. He very simply cursed the vessel the devil employed and made something very clear: this little girl would go on to have a family of her own, a son of her own, and He would end what began that fateful day in Eden. In a phrase, He declared war. "I will put enmity between you and the woman, between your seed and her seed; He shall bruise [crush, break] your head, and you shall bruise His heel."[13] This early judicial sentencing breathes Scripture's first utterance of both the coming Christ and a man John the Beloved would refer to as "the anti-Christ," a man altogether unlike Jesus, yet operating as something of a counterfeit of our blessed King.[14] Even in Eden, we knew the Son of Man was coming. Even in Eden, we knew this fallen age had numbered days. Our merciful God had already devised a means to absolve us from our stupidity.

Deceiving the crafted companion, the crown of creation, was the first slimy task executed by this adversary we'd come to know as the "accuser of the brethren,"[15] who'd managed to steal dominion from mankind. Time would prove this cunning serpent a thief through to the bone, who would seek to steal till Kingdom come.[16] The sentences served to the man and woman were declarations of consequence above much else. The vibrant world Adam and Eve had known had just come under the death they drank; work would become harder, more futile,

---

13   Genesis 3:15
14   1 John 2:18,22; 4:3
15   Revelation 12:10
16   See Matthew 4:6; John 10:10; 12:31; 2 Corinthians 4:4

and less satisfying. Eve's emotional boundaries would blur, and the desire of the feminine heart would now be yoked to the man's. The painful complexities of heterosexual relationship started here, and we have Eve to thank. Life as they had known it was over; our exile from Eden began with the loss of all her luxuries. Yet, the LORD did not hesitate to craft a covering for these exiles; the first literal death in creation, which stopped a beating heart and emptied a set of full lungs, was not the woman. It wasn't the man. It wasn't the snake. It was the animal whose own skins became Adam and Eve's clothes to temper their shame.[17] For all their effort, every other worldview and religion fails to explain why mankind is the only creature on the planet who fashions coverings for its frame. This is the first time the LORD would provide a sacrifice; it would certainly not be the last.

The man hadn't named his wife Eve until they started their sojourning away from God. To name a dying woman *"life"* as she enters exile is nothing short of ironic, but it remains prophetic. God had promised them a Son, and they clung to His word. Death may have begun its reign, but its days were numbered. This wellspring of defiant hope saturated the dreams of fallen mankind, beginning then to rely on the provision and promises of God. Years of confusion, rivalry, and bloodshed would yet pass before men and women of dust and blood would call upon His name.[18] Still, we would call and He would come; when He did in flesh, He would face His own battery of perverted truths and temptations. The first Adam relied on his own self-sufficiencies. The second Adam did not.[19]

---

17 See Genesis 3:21
18 See Genesis 4:26
19 John 5:19-47; 6:35-40; 8:28-19; Romans 5:14-19

CHAPTER THIRTEEN

The Washing Word

IN WHAT IS OFTEN REFERRED TO as the "High Priestly prayer," recorded in John 17, Jesus began His last prayer before His betrayal and arrest with this premise: everything He had done since that "silent night" in Bethlehem, and everything He was about to go through, was to this end: to give eternal life to the men and women given by the Father to the Son. He immediately defined it, for our sakes, with this: "This is eternal life, that they know You the only true God, and Jesus Christ, whom You have sent."[1] Paul would later expound on this mystery, that the Trinity had orchestrated the affair in such a way that these people enlightened in the knowledge of God would then display His wisdom through their witness to the cosmos.[2] It is not unfair to say the foundational purpose and premise of our salvation is a cognitive shift in who we believe and know our Maker to be.

We are souls of minds, wills, and emotions knit to the physical frames of our bodies, and our behaviors are the fruit of the thoughts which take root in our minds.[3] It isn't only important to think rightly about God because it is an injustice against Him to think wrongly of Him; it is critical we think rightly about God because our beliefs infuse and influence our decisions and behaviors. Our ability to walk according

---
1 John 17:2-3
2 Ephesians 3:8-11
3 Proverbs 23:7; Philippians 4:9

to His laws (see Psalm 119) has everything to do with the worldview shaping our inspirations. This is why something like Psalm 27:4 is so important: "One thing have I asked of the LORD, that I will seek after; that I may dwell in the house of the LORD all the days of my life, to gaze upon the beauty of the LORD and to inquire (meditate) in His temple." The human heart obeys that which it desires. Desiring God is crucial to knowing God, and knowing God is impossible without desiring Him. Jesus makes this possible.[4]

"And you, who were once alienated and hostile in mind, doing evil deeds, He has now reconciled in His body of flesh by His death, in order to present you holy and blameless and above reproach before Him."[5] It took the walking Word of God to create a path for us to travel down—hedged in and narrow it may be—to be "transformed by the renewing of [our] mind" along the way.[6] Just as "it is not what enters a man that defiles him," and religious leaders were condemned by the Judge of the Ages as "whitewashed tombs" serving as aesthetically beautiful homes for corpses- we have to understand the primacy of our interior life in the Holy Spirit's agenda to sanctify us in order to fully submit to it.[7] Our very minds must match that of Christ's to be truly conformed into His image, and He is committed to this end[8]— but the disparity between where we begin after Eden and where we're going in Jesus could not be a sharper contrast.

When James (the one who wrote the book in the Bible named after him, historically considered to be the biological half-brother of Jesus) colored in this contrast for us, he didn't mince words. "Wisdom from below"—the best we can come up with for all our worldviews, philosophies, ideologies, advice and Twitter feeds—is "earthly, unspiritual, demonic," a cesspool for "jealousy and selfish ambition." Where jealousy and self-seeking exist, so do "disorder and every evil thing."[9] Every evil thing. Conversely, "wisdom from above is first pure, then peaceable, gentle, open to reason, full of mercy and good fruits, impartial and sincere."[10] This is heaven's divine recourse for

---

4 Proverbs 1:7; 1 John 4:19
5 Colossians 1:21-22
6 Matthew 7:13-14; Romans 12:2
7 Matthew 15:11; 23:27
8 Romans 8:29; Philippians 1:6; 2:5
9 James 3:16, mostly ESV but with an NASB inclusion.
10 James 3:17

our thought lives and all the actions they permeate. A "harvest of righteousness is sown in peace by those who make peace."[11] For all the philosophies and pagan ideologies we've developed through the course of human history, none have been capable of explaining the sources and seedbeds for good and evil, because we are by ourselves altogether incapable of properly diagnosing our hearts as they are: deceitful, and desperately wicked. Who can know it?[12] We are vulnerable to our own self-spun confusions.

Living in the darkness of our own depraved discrepancies, short of a holy intervention, enslaves us to our fallen, fleshly natures. It is a pit we cannot crawl out of; a cage we cannot break our way out of, and mud we cannot clean off of ourselves. We're not left without examples of "every evil thing." Here are a few: adultery, fornication, uncleanness, lewdness, idolatry, sorcery, hatred, contention, jealousy, outbursts of wrath, selfish ambitions, dissension, heresy, envy, murder, drunkenness, revelries, sodomy, theft, covetousness, reviling, extortion, perverted passion, evil desire, cowardice, unbelief, and lying, just for a start.[13] It seems as though everything Jesus rebuked and warned against in Matthew 5-7's beloved "Sermon on the Mount," all the works and passions of the flesh, can be found anchored in James' diagnosis: bitterness and a swollen ego. Murder is the fruit of a root of anger. Anger is sown by what seed? Bitterness and self-seeking. Adultery? Same seed. Unbelief? Also the same seed. Dissension? Community fractures? Robbery? False doctrine? Drunkenness? Manipulation? Fighting? Sexual immorality? All are grounded in bitter envy and self-seeking pursuits. Why did Saul turn on David? He envied him.[14] James could identify bitterness and jealousy in one breath because bitterness is the lashing out of a calloused heart grieving over what we think we deserve. It is no wonder Paul pointed to Jesus' selflessness in Philippians 2 and told us to "have this mind in us also."[15] Those words aren't a light suggestion. They're a lifeline: Prefer people above yourself so you don't get drunk on the seductive doctrine of wayward spirits.

---

11 James 3:18
12 Jeremiah 17:9
13 Matthew 15:18-19; 1 Corinthians 3:3; 6:9-10; Galatians 5:19-21; Ephesians 5:3-4; Colossians 3:5
14 1 Samuel 18:6-9
15 Philippians 2:5

By grace through faith, we can call upon the name of the Lord and know our cry reaches a listening ear and capable hand.[16] We do not have to walk by the flesh.[17] We need not be beholden to confusion and bitterness and "every evil thing."[18] We can get lifted out of the pit. We can get liberated from the cage. We can get the mud washed off of us with the full force of a hose rigged to a fire hydrant. "For you were called to freedom, brothers. Only do not use your freedom as an opportunity for the flesh, but through love serve one another. For the whole law is fulfilled in one word: 'You shall love your neighbor as yourself.' But if you bite and devour one another, watch out that you are not consumed by one another."[19]

"But I say, walk by the Spirit, and you will not gratify the desires of the flesh. For the desires of the flesh are against the Spirit, and the desires of the Spirit are against the flesh, for they are opposed to each other, to keep you from doing the things you want to do. But if you are led by the Spirit, you are not under the law….the fruit of the Spirit is love, joy, peace, patience, kindness, goodness, faithfulness, gentleness, self-control… if we live by the Spirit, let us also walk by the Spirit. Let us not become conceited, provoking one another, envying one another."[20]

Our transformation comes by the Word of the Lord.[21]

Our transformation hinges on the integrity of the Word of the Lord.

Our transformation gives birth to our agreement with the Word of the Lord.

Our bondage, propensity to sin, slavery to the "flesh," and ongoing threat to our safety and security since mankind's exile from Eden are not the bad behaviors rattled off in the lists above in and of themselves; rather, they are anchored in the same accusation leveled against the nature and character of God then that is leveled against Him in our minds now: "Did He really say?" Is His Word really true? Accurate? Fair? Just? Binding?

---

16   Numbers 11:23; Isaiah 59:1
17   See Galatians 5:16
18   James 3:16
19   Galatians 5:13-15
20   Galatians 5:16-18, 22-26
21   See 2 Corinthians 4:6

The more we question and accuse Him, the more we roll around in the mud, and the more the cesspool of wickedness within us devours, conceives, and births these shattering iniquities. Inevitably, we become confused by our continued dances with old demons. Why do we continue to engage in sin?[22] What if we're frauds who aren't actually even saved? When Jesus purges the foul stains of sin and treason from our souls, He does so by the finality of what He purchased with His own blood on Calvary and by the slow and steady process of sanctification in this age—reshaping the clay of our hearts, minds, wills, and emotions into His Image.[23] We'll get better bodies when He returns.[24] This requires daily believing—to "believe, and keep on believing"[25]—that He is, and that He rewards those who seek Him out beyond the lying narrative of this "present evil age."[26]

Therefore, eternal life is to know Him. "Abiding" means we know Him internally, to such depths and degrees that the knowledge of Jesus literally rewires the way we think. It thus bears consequence on even the way we react when our relationships and calendars and bank accounts and bodies throw whatever they do at us. Is He still good? Is He still strong enough to save us? Is He still coming? Is He who He said He is? Is He? Our confidence in His nature, His character, the core of who He is comes only by faith, and faith by hearing the Word of the LORD.[27] He intervenes in our lives by and through His Word, and His Word is who He is. Jesus is the manifest and Incarnate Word of the LORD[28]—therefore Jesus Himself is our intervention. He is our transformation. He is our buoy to keep us above water when we are "tossed with tempest,"[29] and the arm that pulls us out of the water when we're drowning. He is the clarity in our confusion, the fort we run to when our trenches are overrun, the guardian of our souls, and the compass who counsels us through the maps of our lives.[30]

When we reflect on the birth of the Galilean, the Word of God

---

22 See Romans 7:13-25
23 See Genesis 1:26-27; Romans 8:29
24 See 1 Corinthians 15:20-23; 1 Thessalonians 4:13-17
25 See 1 John 5:4-5
26 Hebrews 11:6; Galatians 4
27 Romans 10:17
28 John 1:1,14
29 Isaiah 54:11
30 See Psalm 12:6; 18:2; 54:4

incarnate, we can so easily and blissfully get lost in the many names (natures) of the Triune God revealed to us in the glowing face of a Man who seemed so ordinary, we'd likely have passed Him on the street without realizing the glory He'd forfeit to stand beside us.[31] Yet it is right we are mesmerized. It is right to beg His Name of Him, "seeing it is beautiful."[32] It is right to journey through Advent to meet Him at the manger, sink our knees into the mud beside Him, and stare in wonder at the humility required for the God of glory to find Himself in diapers.

Our history began with this mud and dirt and dust; He is so fond of forming new things with it He used it to give new eyes to a blind man.[33] I hope I never get used to the idea that when the Word intervened for death-bound traitors, He did so as a "father who knows our frame and remembers we are but dust."[34] He made His move with mercy for our mess. He didn't forget the dirt He made us out of. He didn't hold us to a higher standard than our limitations allowed. We believed bad things, did dumb things, and made a mess we could not get ourselves out of. He didn't berate us, abandon us, or unequivocally condemn us. He just got in the dirt with us. He lived all our limitations just like us. (How He did it for over thirty years without ever sinfully losing His temper still just makes me dumbstruck.)

We made a mess in our mud, and Heaven's answer was to get into the manger.

James and Paul both would lean on this counter-intuitive example later as directive on how to treat your believing buddy when they get entangled in some kind of sin-drunk stupidity—because we're being conformed into the image of the compassionate Father who causes a famine to pull us out of a pig pen, push us home, and then runs off the porch to meet us in the road.[35] Paul pulled from this as a model for marriage: "husbands, love your wives, give up your life for them,

---

[31] Isaiah 53:2; 2 Corinthians 4:6; Philippians 2:6-7; for the chosen use of the word "forfeit," see "Hymn" by Brooke Fraser

[32] Judges 13:18; I recommend Hillsong's "What A Beautiful Name" get stuck in your head.

[33] Genesis 2:7; John 9:6

[34] Psalm 103:14

[35] Luke 15:11-32; James 5:19-20

just like Jesus did for you, so that He could wash you with the water of His Word and clean you up for the resurrection."[36]

It is an intimate intervention. There is no way to stay clean or dry when you're giving someone a bath—not a child, not an ill or handicapped relative, not a heroin addict, and not even your Labrador. Giving someone a good wash means you get in the process with them. It means you get soaked the same. It means you get their dirt on you. This is what Jesus did in the Incarnation. He got your dirt on Him and He didn't get mad about it. He took on the form of His form, bottled Himself into a dusty frame that looks just like the rest of us made out of dirt and blood, and got in our mess with us. "The Word made flesh"[37] got all up in our junk, and emphatically declared who God is and what He is like—that He is patient. Gracious. Meek. Longsuffering. Just. Kind. Humble. Hopeful. Forgiving. Wise. Compassionate. Generous. Merciful. Abounding in loving kindness.[38]

Our truest transformations come through Jesus' delicate responses to our vulnerabilities. In mercy, He stoops far below what He deserves to serve us by means we most certainly do not deserve. We get clean simply because He wants to clean us. It is His intrinsic goodness we rely on and it is His consistent commitment to "do us good"[39] we lean on. We have nothing but His hand to hold us.

Hours before Jesus sweat blood in Gethsemane praying for you and me, He knelt to wash twenty-four dirty, unmanicured, foul-smelling feet.[40] I can only imagine how the twelve disciples, who'd followed Him so far and seen Him do such incredible things, would have reacted. We know Jesus had to disarm Peter's false humility and reassure the young man of His sufficiency. But what did John think? Was he also surprised, or did he have a "go figure" moment? Did Thomas think, "But wait... You're the guy who controls the weather and turned water into wine..."? Did any of them think, "But did it have to be our feet?!"? More than anything, what on earth did Judas think? He left the room an hour or two later to sell Jesus to bloodthirsty

---

36   Ephesians 5:25-32
37   John 1:14
38   Exodus 34:6-7; Matthew 11:29; I Corinthians 13:4-8
39   Jeremiah 32:40-41
40   See John 13

conspirators. Was his heart so calloused by that point that he just got offended at Jesus' humility?

Is yours?

The One who controls the weather, turns water into wine, makes blind eyes see, and heals handicapped bodies is the One who authors your salvation. He's the One who judges your filth, intervenes, makes a way, and makes you clean. So when He calls you clean, do you (like Peter) still feel like more needs to be done? Do you resent His authority in the conversation at all? Or do you just continue to agree with the truth of your pre-bath status that you're unclean and foul?

Agreement with accusation against ourselves (and others), in light of Jesus' death and resurrection, isn't just cute false humility (another, more subtle, form of pride). It is a dirty and demonic libel against the character of Jesus. Here's why:

The prophet Zechariah had a powerful vision of Joshua, Israel's high priest at the time.[41] In the prophet's vision, the priest was standing before the Angel of the LORD (again, not just an angel), with Satan (Hebrew for "the accuser" or "the adversary") at his right hand, poised to accuse the priest. It is a judicial setting. The defendant is in front of the Judge—and stuck next to the prosecuting attorney. You might read this and wonder where the defense attorney is in the scene.

Keep reading.

Joshua's clothes are dirty. He's not only in court in wrinkled, unwashed clothes standing in front of His Judge. He's also a man with a history of sin, standing in front of the sinless One. Jesus and Joshua both know what this man has done—in fact, it's fair to say Joshua knows a little bit, but enough. Jesus literally knows full well He could fairly pronounce a guilty sentence then and there. Neither of them need the prosecuting attorney to make his case. Here is a man appointed to ministry he is not qualified for. He's been appointed to represent the nation before their LORD, and even he can't get his act together. His nation sure can't. Still, before Joshua's accuser can point to his filthy garments—let alone begin to read off his record—the Judge speaks up.

---

41 See Zechariah 3

He rebukes the accuser.

"The LORD rebuke you, O Satan! The LORD who has chosen Jerusalem rebuke you! Is this not a brand plucked from the fire?"[42]

Jesus didn't need to hear the case against Joshua, and Joshua didn't need a defense attorney. Jesus was his defense attorney. He didn't need Satan to point out that Joshua's clothing was inappropriate and his covering was grossly insufficient. And He didn't let the devil get a word in edgewise. We can interject some Pauline theology here: chapter eight of his letter to the Romans is what happens when Paul's delight in God's unwarranted advocacy on our behalves flows through pen to meet his parchment. "And we know that all things work together for good to those who love God, to those who are called according to His purpose. For whom He foreknew, He also predestined to be conformed to the image of His Son, that He might be the firstborn among many brethren. Moreover whom He predestined, these He also called; whom He called, these He also justified; and whom He justified, these He also glorified."[43]

The conversation in the courtroom wasn't about Joshua's sinfulness and insufficiency. It was about Jesus' sinlessness and Jesus' sufficiency. "Yes, devil, I know exactly who this man is—but do you? Is he not a brand plucked from the fire? Did I not choose him? Did I not intervene on My own accord and pull him from the fire?" Am I not strong enough to finish what I started? We all have "before Christ" testimonies we have to lay down at the cross—what really troubles us is we'll all have "after Christ" testimonies, when we really botch it because we know better. It's one thing to sin before your eyes are opened to the fact of sin. It's another to deliberately choose it when you know what it costs Jesus. What do you say when you throw yourself back into the mud? What case can you make for pardoning? All that matters in the courtroom is who your Advocate is. Jesus' achievements on the Cross either finished the work, or they didn't. If, truly, "it is finished," it is finished. Your Advocate will see you through to the Day of Reckoning.[44]

When you realize your clothes are dirty and your covering doesn't

---

42 Zechariah 3:2
43 Romans 8:28-30, NKJV
44 1 Corinthians 1:7-8; 1 John 2:1

cover you the way it's supposed to, exposure is the best kind of shipwreck. Stark vulnerability in the courtroom that matters for eternity strips away whatever platform or position or role you have in life—none of it matters when you're that aware of your incredible ability to condemn yourself and your absolute inability to save yourself.

Before the devil could condemn Joshua, Jesus intervened. Before the devil could refute Jesus' declaration, Jesus advocated for Joshua. He took the man's dirty clothes and poor covering and gave him a clean, white robe sufficient both to cover and qualify him to stand before the Judge and not die.

Joshua couldn't do that, and he didn't. Near as we know, he didn't even bother or have the audacity to ask for it. Jesus just did it because He is a very capable Savior and a very merciful Judge who is both just and the justifier of those who have faith.[45] This is good news for all of us—the best news. It is our testimony. "As such were some of you. But you were washed, you were sanctified, you were justified in the name of the Lord Jesus Christ and by the Spirit of our God."[46]

White garments are another recurring theme throughout Scripture. At its end, the apostle John received a vision himself in which he saw the saints of God, those bought and washed by the blood of the Lamb.[47] The Revelation of Jesus ends with the full and final restoration of all things destroyed and corroded by the lie of Eden's snake. Human history will see its darkest days before the Lord's return, and we'll see the absolute contrast of our sin and godlessness against His truth and glory. All of us—"such were some of us"—will see all we could have become without the cleansing flood from Immanuel's veins, and instead of receiving the severity of our guilty sentence, we will shine something like jasper in the Kingdom of our Father.[48]

It is in our best interests now to just be His children and believe Him.

---

[45] Romans 3:26
[46] 1 Corinthians 6:11
[47] See Revelation; verses 7:13-14 address it specifically for those who've survived the tribulation before the Lord's return.
[48] Matthew 13:43

Section Five

Light of the World

*"In Him was life, and the life was the light of men.
And the light shines in the darkness,
and the darkness did not comprehend it."*

John 1:4–5

CHAPTER FOURTEEN

The Blood-Soaked Garden

BEFORE THE WORD EVER UTTERED "let there be light," the Word had committed to an Incarnated life bound to the shape and form of those who would bear His holy Image. Jesus is the Lamb "slain before the foundations of the world."[1] The star over Bethlehem was in His eyes before light ever broke the cosmic darkness. Golgotha's blood-soaked soil was part of His dream when He divided oceans with continents. The cross of Jesus is why He made this age with this world and all us players on this particular stage. This is about Christ and Him crucified. It's about the slain Son of God receiving an inheritance from His Father appropriately proportional to who He is and what He deserves. It's about the wife of the Lamb becoming an "equally yoked" partner and "suitable helpmate" for her Husband. That's His dream for us. We absolutely do not deserve any of it. We absolutely do not deserve any of Him.

Despite—and in spite of—many of our efforts to the contrary, He will conform those He predestined to be transferred into the kingdom of His beloved Son, into the image of the His beloved Son.[2] He is committed to committing us to the end.[3] He won't drop the ball or let us fall through the cracks. When we really botch it, He'll roll up

---

[1] Romans 8:29; Ephesians 1:4; 3:9-11; 1 Peter 1:19-20; Revelation 13:8
[2] Matthew 3:17; 17:5; Mark 9:7; Luke 9:35; Colossians 1:13-14
[3] See 1 Corinthians 1:6-8

His sleeves and get to work to rewrite our stories in crimson ink. The halls of Heaven will be lined with shining trophies of the amazing grace that saves such a wretch like you and me. Our sins and stupid decisions in this age will be distant memories, stories told in the resurrection with tears and laughter over dinner with the rest of the Body of Jesus—including some of the people who hurt us most deeply, and many of the people we wounded in all the worst ways. Gratitude will mark all our ages to come, and we'll see our stories for all they are and the full extent of wickedness for all the stupid things we did.

Until then, we undergo the painful process of sanctifying conformation. We will resemble Jesus when this is all said and done. In the meantime, we are carried by grace through faith—the faith of the patriarch Abraham, the "father of our faith in the God who raises the dead."[4] We cannot cheat our way through the process, and neither could he. Perhaps the most painful day in his life was hearing he had to take the life of his son of promise; his son of covenant. Genesis 22 records a time "God tested Abraham"[5]—by commanding him to drag his darling son up a hill and kill him as a human sacrifice.

If we misunderstand the nature of this test, we will misunderstand the nature of our Father in heaven. We'll misunderstand the nature of the cross and we'll call it something like "cosmic child abuse."[6]

Our Father in heaven is good and only good. There is no darkness in His light.[7]

The cross of Jesus was not cosmic child abuse.

Abraham was being discipled by his good Father. He was being led through life by his Good Shepherd. This man who would become the father for all who call upon the name of the God who raises the dead had to become like the good Father, who would be willing to let His Son die for sake of sovereign strategy. Abraham didn't understand it. He just knew God was good enough to be trusted when details were dark and things were difficult. He knew Isaac would live again,

---

[4] See Hebrews 11:17-19
[5] Genesis 22:1
[6] This phraseology has recently emerged to reject the doctrine of Jesus' substitutionary atonement on our behalves.
[7] James 1:17

because God wouldn't renege on His promises that hinged on Isaac's survival.

So in Genesis 22, we see the father of the covenant lead his son of the covenant up a hill in Moriah and place his son on a stone for sacrifice. We see the son of the covenant allow his father to bind his hands and lay him out on the rock. He didn't fight back. I don't know why. I don't know if Abraham had to knock Isaac out from behind, or if the boy just submitted to the process. I don't know. What I do know is this: the LORD never intended for Isaac's life to be taken that day, and He intervened right when He needed to. Both the father and the son of the Everlasting Covenant would've walked down the hill of Moriah different men than had walked up earlier that day. Abraham's character as the father of the faith had been conformed into the image of the Father who was willing to let His beloved Son die in the stead of sinful men like Abraham and David and Moses and you and me. Our lives will display the message and image we are crafted to carry and emulate. Abraham and Isaac were no exception. Neither are we.

Later, the Son of Man and God and David spent His last evening in a garden shaking with dread, knowing what would meet Him on Moriah in the morning. We must be clear: no one took His life. He laid it down.[8] And, like any reasonable mind, He wasn't seeking martyrdom. He didn't delight in suffering. He wanted the joy set before Him on the other side of pain, trial, and testing. He didn't want the cross. He wanted what He'd gain afterwards. Ultimately, He wanted to glorify the name of His Father.

In a moment of holy despair, He uttered so we could hear: "Father, if it is Your will, take this cup away from Me; nevertheless not My will, but Yours, be done."[9] If this degree of suffering and scourging was outside the will of His Father, He wanted to avoid it and trusted His Father to guard Him from unnecessary torture. If it was within the will of His Father, however, He trusted Him. He didn't question His Father's goodness, sovereignty, or trustworthiness.

Here we must pause and consider what we believe when the lights are off. When we are in our own Gethsemanes, when we are facing our own Golgothas, what do we believe about our Father?

---

[8] John 10:17-18
[9] John 17:42

Consider Jesus.[10] As He shook and sweat blood, His Father did not take Golgotha's cup away from Him. Imagine what this did to Him as a Dad. But He did send a friend to strengthen His Son, much like Jonathan found David in a moment of his deepest despair and fear of death. "Remember who you are and what the LORD has made you for," said the one born to the throne, to the one actually appointed to it. "He will see you through."[11] Similarly, when David's Son despaired of death, "an angel appeared to Him from heaven, strengthening Him."[12] Maybe he reminded Him of the Jerusalem to come.[13] Maybe he didn't say a word. Maybe he just sat with the Son in the quiet dark, and offered Him the ministry of presence in the midst of incredible pain.

Whatever he did, Jesus' Father sent that angel. He did not leave His Son alone in Gethsemane.

He will not leave you alone in yours.

---

10 See Hebrews 3:1
11 See 1 Samuel 23:16-17
12 Luke 22:43
13 See Revelation 21:9-10

CHAPTER FIFTEEN

SOBER RESPONSIBILITY

IT IS A KINGDOM PRINCIPLE THAT "to whom much is given, much is required."[1] This is true of everything we have been given in our lives; "every good and perfect gift" comes to us from the hand of our Father.[2] He is the One who gives the power to make wealth,[3] and as such, our use of finances is a stewardship issue. Our hospitality is a stewardship issue. Our humble distribution of knowledge is a stewardship issue. Our posture in positions of privilege is an issue of stewardship—and to whom much has been given, much will be required.

We're already living in an incredible hour of human suffering, on a scale beyond most of history and with a momentum outpacing even the greatest catastrophes in our history books. If Jesus' return is preceded by a time of trouble so great He had to "cut short" its allotted days, lest no one survive[4] (which I believe is the consistent testimony of the patriarchs, psalmists, prophets, and pioneers of the "one new man"[5]) that must shape and influence the way we decide to live our lives. We each have numbered days like designated dollars,

---

1 Luke 12:48
2 James 1:17
3 See Deuteronomy 8:18
4 Matthew 24:22
5 Ephesians 2:15

and we spend one every twenty-four hours. What are we spending our lives on? Both our legacies for following generations and our rewards in the coming ages are at stake. We cannot responsibly regard these truths and yet decide to live for ourselves today. If Jesus is who He says He is, and if there is in fact a coming resurrection, Day of judgment, and if there really are eternal implications on what we say and do in this age (and there are),[6] then these truths and issues shadowing over our tomorrow bear a tremendous weight on the decisions we make today.

From dust we come, and to dust we return. Everything we gain between the days we're born and die is ultimately on loan. We must discern what we've been given and prayerfully pursue the best and highest way to invest and spend it—our time, our money, our love, our service. In speaking of living in light of eternity, Paul admonished us to navigate our lives with drunk spirits and sober minds[7]—meaning we abide in communion with Him who lives inside us, carefully aware of the world we're in, to be "in it but not of it."[8] It is another way of Jesus' sage counsel to proceed gentle as doves but wise as serpents.[9] We have not been left without a substantially detailed worldview and its implications. What is up to us is how we then live with the knowledge of it.

When James outlined his pastoral case against disillusionment and hypocrisy, he boiled it all down to one directive: "visit widows and orphans in their distress, to keep oneself unspotted from the world."[10] As "salt of the earth and light of the world,"[11] we are stewards of truth and hope in a dark and dying world. Why would we waste our time and energy trying to "get away with" as much as we could while being held responsible for as little as possible? Are we children of our Father, or are we carrying our "Get Out Of Jail Free" cards for our own sakes' down the track? Do we bow the knee to the Servant of all,[12] or don't we?

---

6   See Matthew 6:1,4,6,18; 12:36
7   See Ephesians 5:18
8   John 17:15-16
9   Matthew 10:16
10 James 1:27
11 Matthew 5:13-16
12 See Mark 9:35; Philippians 2:5-11

If we've any zeal for holiness and a life of purity—knowing we'll inherit the kingdom of our Father[13]—our best practice is to serve those who can't repay us anything in return. With an epidemic of fatherlessness, the West is full of single mothers and kids without dads in the home. With a hemorrhaging refugee crisis, we are not without opportunities to give what we have to serve those who have nothing. This is true of the finances we've been entrusted with, the truth we've been entrusted with, and the measure of grace given to us with which we're to serve the Body.

Before it describes a "virtuous wife,"[14] Proverbs 31 begins with an oracle from the Queen Mother to her son Lemuel. Jewish legend suspects this otherwise anonymous character may be Solomon, making Bathsheba the woman of wisdom here, but there's no real way to tell at this point in history. Without knowing who exactly dispersed these words, or what so burdened her to sit her son down and make sure he heard her, we're able to feel the grief in her heart as she admonished her son to rule his throne well and fairly—requiring he do so soberly.[15]

Lemuel's position of privilege meant he had things others didn't have but desperately needed. If he irresponsibly went through his days drunk on his own desires and the pleasures afforded him in the highest office of the land, he would invariably withhold necessities from his people and abuse his power. "What?" his mother asked.[16] "What, my son? Son of my womb? Son of my vows?" Any mother can remember realizing she is pregnant; here she reminds him there is a broader story he was born into, and an integrity he is held to by virtue of his birth and lineage. "Do not spend your days and strength on that which destroys kings." At whatever age he took his father's throne, he was young enough that she needed him to know certain things would make his crown erode. Others would make it last—and it had everything to do with how he stewarded what he had been given. He did not earn his throne. He was born into it.

We need to hear the Queen Mother with the same tender sobriety she first spoke these words. If you know the name of Jesus, have

---

13   See Luke 12:32
14   Proverbs 31:10
15   See Proverbs 31:1-9
16   See Proverbs 31:2

access to a Bible in your own language, own more than one article of clothing, and have any money in your bank account, you're already at an advantage. Don't get lost in politics of a shifting government and fluid economy. Policies are important, but they do not define our days and they will mean little to nothing in the world after the grave.

We need to see she isn't advocating for prohibition (though certainly she cautions us all against a life of drunkenness), but instead puts her hands on both our cheeks, holds us still, and forces us to look her in the eye. "Do not waste your life," she tells us. "Do not spend what you have on yourself."

She is not simply instructing a wealthy man to pursue a tax deduction. She pivots seamlessly: Give your wine to the man who needs to forget his sorrow, and go to bat for him. "Open your mouth for the speechless, in the cause of all who are appointed to die. Open your mouth, judge righteously, and plead the cause of the poor and needy."[17] Speak for those who can't speak. Advocate for those disadvantaged by war, poverty, "deliver those who are drawn to death, and hold back those who are stumbling to the slaughter."[18]

"If you say, 'well, we didn't know this,' does not He who weighs the hearts consider it?"[19] If you skip past the suffering in the world around you, either on the other end of your block or on the other side of the world, do you intend to tell the Judge on that Day that you just "didn't know" about it, like He didn't see every time you changed the channel or just kept scrolling? He knows what you know. He knows what you have. He knows what you've been given. And He will call you to give an account for what you did with it all.[20]

Privilege is not a right. If you were born into an affluent demographic, the Lord will see what you did to serve those who weren't. Why? Because He serves those who have less. The poor and disenfranchised have no greater advocate than the Ruler of Heaven and Earth. Certainly many things will shock us as He sets up His Jerusalem-based government in the millennium—few more than how many who

---

17   Proverbs 31:8-9
18   Proverbs 24:11
19   Proverbs 24:12
20   See Matthew 25:14-30

are now "last will be first," and how many "first" accustomed to so much will be assigned to the back of the line.[21]

We are made in His Image, and we're built to bear it even if the reflection in this age is dimmer than it will be in the next.[22] When we are made aware of poverty and pull nothing out of what we have in our pockets, it's like we left the mirror and forgot what we saw.[23] To whom much is given, much will be required. When we are informed of how many people are living without the knowledge of Jesus, but somehow are entirely comfortable hoarding the Gospel within our borders, it's like spitting on the Word that made His name known. To whom much is given, much will be required. When we see opportunities to engage and effect change in this fallen world, we must wonder what led us to believe Lemuel was given a crown so he could white-knuckle the wealth of his nation. We know our lives are like grass that grows today and withers or gets mowed down tomorrow.[24] As the tireless abolitionist and politician William Wilberforce indicted his fellow members of Parliament, he ended his case against slavery: "Having heard all this, you may choose to look the other way—but you can never again say you did not know."[25]

---

21   See Matthew 20:16; Mark 9:35; 10:31; Luke 13:30
22   See 1 Corinthians 13:12
23   See James 1:22-25
24   See Isaiah 40:6-8; James 4:14
25   Close of a speech in House of Commons (1791), as quoted in *Once Blind: The Life of John Newton* (2008) by Kay Marshall Strom, p. 225.

CHAPTER SIXTEEN

INTERCEDE (V):
TO INTERVENE

FEW TRUTHS CONVEY THE AUTHENTICITY of the Gospel like the appalling servant-hearted nature of King Jesus, who explicitly took on the form of His form to show us the Father in Heaven.[1] The One who tells the waves how far they're allowed to travel around the globe[2] also told blindness when its days were up,[3] stopped stones before they left bloodthirsty hands,[4] advocated for little kids,[5] and dropped the hammer on chauvinists bent to publicly revile a young woman.[6] Our magnificent Maker, who cannot look at the stars He made without insulting His dignity as the High and Lofty One, made Himself into a walking mirror of dirt and blood just so He could kneel in it and wash it off our feet,[7] just so He could have a rusty nail pierce His own to splintery planks and suffocate to save His traitors.[8]

1   John 14:1-11; 17:6
2   Job 38:11
3   Mark 8:22-25; 10:46-52; John 9:1-7
4   John 8:1-11
5   Matthew 19:14; Luke 18:16
6   This happened on two occasions: a "certain woman" in Luke 7:36-50, and Lazarus' sister Mary in Matthew 26:6-13; Mark 14:3-9; John 12:1-8
7   Isaiah 57:15; Psalm 113:4-6; John 13:1-15
8   Romans 5:7-10

While these characteristics of Jesus are wonderful and illuminate His beauty, we would do both our hearts and His reputation a disservice if we whitewashed the nature of His actions. This was an intervention. Wrath is coming, and heaven intervened.[9] When we were drunk on delusion and making deliriously sinful decisions—and *enjoying* them—Jesus hounded us down, found us out, took us home, and He still wrestles us through our tantrums while we work our way through the tormenting fog of withdrawal.[10] Regeneration is a *work*, and thank God He will finish what He started.[11] Redemption is *costly*, and thank God He didn't hesitate when He saw the bill our sobriety would cost. His heart didn't drop to His gut when He realized it would cost *His own blood*. The penny never had to drop for Jesus. Rather, the LORD ordained His own path to the Place of the Skull before He ever uttered "Let there be light."[12] It is worth our time to reflect on these words from Charles Spurgeon:

> *"Jesus' sheep are His by conquest. What a battle He had in us before we would be won! How long a siege He laid to our hearts! How often He sent us terms of capitulation! But we barred our gates, and fenced our walls against Him. Do we not remember that glorious hour when He carried our hearts by storm? When He placed His cross against the wall, and scaled our ramparts, planting on our strongholds the blood-red flag of His omnipotent mercy? Yes, we are, indeed, the conquered captives of His omnipotent love. Thus chosen, purchased, and subdued, the rights of our divine possessor are inalienable: we rejoice that we can never be our own; and we desire, day by day, to do His will, and show forth His glory."*[13]

Loving Jesus means living like Jesus. Obedience to Jesus looks like a willing vessel of clay leaning into the formative hands of our Potter, so committed to conforming us to His beloved Son. By presenting a walking witness of the Wounded One, we "fill up what is lacking of

---

9   Matthew 3:7; Luke 3:7
10 Psalm 23:6; Isaiah 53:12
11 Philippians 1:6
12 Revelation 13:8; Genesis 1:3
13 Spurgeon, Charles H. "The Lord's Portion is His People (Deuteronomy 32:9)." *Morning and Evening,* (1886). November 15th reading.

the afflictions of Christ,"[14] so when we *tell* people about the crucified King of glory, they *see* the manifest message of His name embodied in our own lives.

When He paid our ransom on Calvary's hill and the Son of promise bled out on Moriah, Jesus sealed the warrant for the redemption of His image-bearers: us.[15] We were made to look like Him, the Cross was not Eden's Plan B. He ordained this age of Gethsemanes and Golgothas to purge us of the egos we don't have the right to keep, and turn us into Christians.[16] "Little Christs."[17] Little versions of the matchless Sovereign who didn't mind the toll His reputation took when Mary had to change His diapers.[18]

What rehabilitation professionals refer to as "intervention" is one dimension to the brilliant diamond the Scriptures describe as *intercession*. In fact, the words are nearly two sides of one coin; the latter was a linguistic development from the former. His humiliating incarnation *interceded* for us; and *praise the Lamb* He continues to intercede and intervene for us still.[19] He gets in-between us and our sin.[20] He gets in-between us and our enemies.[21] He gets in-between us and the enemies we make *because* of our sin.[22]

To intercede is to give an incarnate witness of the Incarnate God to a world so stricken by poverty of soul and conscience. Intercession includes and requires prayer. It also demands action, in the same way Jesus prays and contends for our sakes and salvation because He saw the death we deserve and took it upon Himself to *get in the way*. He got in-between us and the bad because He cares. If we are to be "conformed into His image"[23]—and we will be—we will be a people who do the same. People who pray, contend, fast, and *get in the way*.

---

14 Colossians 1:24
15 James 1:18
16 Romans 8:29
17 That's what the word "Christian" means. What a privilege.
18 Philippians 2:5-8
19 Romans 8:34
20 Colossians 3:3
21 Psalm 59:1-2
22 1 Samuel 30 describes the day the LORD ended a season of compromise in David's life—and vindicated David as though he had no guilt. Truly, He delivers simply because He delights in us (Psalm 18:19).
23 Romans 8:29

It is right to adore Jesus. It is appropriate to behave like Him. He is the "great Intercessor," Author of so many divine interventions.[24] It is appropriate, then, that *we* intercede and intervene on behalf of others as well. It is appropriate to "have this mind in us also," and give ourselves to inconvenient and sacrificial service.[25] In like kind, selfish worship insults the sacrificial nature of the God who bled out on Golgotha, and we will plateau and backslide in our own discipleship if we never break through the ceiling of servitude.

This is why fasting without proactively righting societal wrongs so aggravates the heart of the Holy.[26]

This is why "pure and undefiled religion" means you go to bat for people who have no advocates and you empty your own pockets to cover the cost yourself.[27]

This is why He led Jonah all the way to Mosul to warn of the wrath to come and called Hosea to see his wayward wife all the way to their silver anniversary.

This is why He "searches the earth" to find hearts who've pledged their allegiances to Him so He can show the world He has their back.[28]

This is why He is looking for people to "stand in the gap" when the fatal consequences of sin and transgressions are bearing just weight upon the world, as we soak our soil with our own blood.[29]

We turn corners in our own lives when we decisively commit to "have this mind" in us also,[30] much like Hudson Taylor's transformative time on Brighton Beach in the summer of 1865. He recorded afterwards that while in a corporate worship service home in England after spending some preliminary time in China, his stomach turned and he couldn't stay in the room:

> *"Unable to bear the sight of a congregation of a thousand or more Christian people rejoicing in their own security, while*

---

24 Hebrews 12:2
25 Philippians 2:5
26 Isaiah 58:1-7
27 James 1:27
28 2 Chronicles 16:9
29 Ezekiel 22:30; Romans 6:23
30 Philippians 2:5

> *millions were perishing for lack of knowledge, I wandered out on the sands alone, in great spiritual agony; and there the* LORD *conquered my unbelief, and I surrendered myself to God for this service. I told Him that all the responsibility as to issues and consequences must rest with Him; that as His servant, it was mine to obey and to follow Him—His, to direct, to care for, and to guide me and those who might labour with me. Need I say that peace at once flowed into my burdened heart?"*[31]

It is *wrong* to not adore Jesus and it is wrong to refuse and rebel against His purposes—this is the fundamental sin of which we must all repent. To resist the hand of the Potter as He shapes us into disciples of His beautiful Son is to resist the Sovereign of the ages and commit treason against His crown. In these tumultuous days of war, famine, conflict, crisis, and calamity, it is *imperative* we allow Him to trade our calloused, rock-hard hearts for tender, beating organs of flesh healthy enough to pump blood through our frames.[32] Meaning if we see suffering and it doesn't bother us, something is wrong. Soberly, such insensitivity is one of the loudest sirens alarming us we've long since ceased to "abide" and are dangerously far from the Vine.[33] The Word of the LORD calls and commands us to:

> *"Rescue those who are being taken away to death; hold back those who are stumbling to the slaughter. If you say, 'Well, we didn't know,' does not He who weighs your heart perceive it? Does not He who keeps watch over your soul know it, and will He not repay?"*[34]

Opportunities to intercede on someone else's behalf are holy privileges of unrivaled dignity. It is also a safeguard against our own pride, and a guaranteed fast-pass to the heart of Jesus. We are not and will never be more compassionate than Jesus. We will never have a stronger sense of justice or groan for mercy than Jesus—but we *can* rightly represent Him to our hurting world while it finishes its sentence under

---

31 Piper, John. "The ministry of Hudson Taylor," (2004). Accessed July 2017. http://www.desiringgod.org/messages/the-ministry-of-hudson-taylor-as-life-in-christ.
32 Ezekiel 36:26
33 John 15:1-11
34 Proverbs 24:11-12

the sway of the wicked one.[35] We can *only* serve Jesus and others in this way *while we live through* Gethsemanes and Golgothas. We have just this age to suffer in another's stead and serve afflicted, distressed, and impoverished men and women made in His holy image. We have just until the Lord returns to, like Paul, "fill up what is lacking in the afflictions of Christ"[36] and live in a way that allows the poor, needy, and even the yet-unrepentant to peer into the mystery of the suffering Servant.

For all the white noise of news headlines, pundits, and politicians, the seven and a half billion people on the planet desperately need the Word of the LORD.

We cannot pray the Word if we do not know the Word.

We cannot live the Word if we do not know the Word.

We have every opportunity now to declare, by our hands, feet, and tongues, the Word of God as revealed in the face of Jesus of Nazareth.

If we *don't*, how will they ever hear it?[37] If we hear the Word of God and ignore it, we disobey Jesus and deceive ourselves—like we looked in a mirror and then walked away without remembering what we saw.[38]

---

35 John 12:31; 14:30; 2 Corinthians 4:4
36 Colossians 1:24
37 Romans 10:14-15
38 James 1:22-24

CHAPTER SEVENTEEN

THAT OTHERS MAY LIVE

AT THE CORE OF INTERCESSION is a driving commitment to self-sacrificing service for the benefit of others. We see this even within the Trinity, setting the family culture we are adopted into and required to conform to. The Father, Son, and Spirit are the triune God who is One,[1] each member of the Godhead serving the others. The Father gives a kingdom to His Son.[2] The Son receives it and gives it all back to His Father.[3] Jonathan Edwards understood the Holy Spirit as the synergistic delight between the Father and the Son.[4] In this Kingdom, none live for themselves.[5] Theirs is a royal household of both public and private honor, servitude, and blessing. Each is steadfastly committed to the Father's plans, ambitions, and timing.

The diligent practice of "carrying [our] cross[es]"[6] requires a certain death to ourselves every day. If we were to try to resurrect the "old

---

1   Deuteronomy 6:4; Zechariah 14:9; Philippians 1:2; Titus 2:13; Acts 5:3-4
2   Psalm 2:1-12; 110:1-7
3   1 Corinthians 15:24; Hebrews 1:13-14
4   Edwards, Jonathan. "Writings on the Trinity, Grace, and Faith," (1704). WJE Online, Vol. 21. Accessed July 2017. http://edwards.yale.edu/archive?path=aHR0cDovL2Vkd-2FyZHMueWFsZS5lZHUvY2dpLWJpbi9uZXdwaGlsby9nZXRvYmplY3QucGw/Yy4yMDozLndqZW8=.
5   This phrase is attributed to the Moravians of Herrnhut, Germany under Count Zinzendorf's leadership.
6   Matthew 16:24-26; Luke 9:23; 14:27

101

man"[7] left behind in the waters of baptism and blood-stained soil of Golgotha, we'd quickly entangle ourselves again in a war the Spirit was sent to help us settle. It's not worth it. I can't imagine Gomer remembered with fondness the day her husband had to come buy her out of her debts and prostitution *again*.[8] My guess is that she learned over her lifetime she was better off to stay home with the man who gave his name, life, and reputation to her. When we confess the name of Jesus and spend our days living for ourselves, we're crawling back into the cuffs that will once again drag us up to the auctioning block. "It is for freedom Christ set us free,"[9] and we are bound by that freedom. Put simply, we'll serve whoever we serve—either sin or Jesus will be our master.[10] We will never be able to rule ourselves.

Our liberty is found fully in happy service to our happy God, as it is only then we discover the "good works" we were fashioned for and the calling we're meant to walk worthy of.[11] It is no wonder, then, that modern psychology can see a direct correlation between deliberate acts of kindness and mental health. Community service is understood to be a vital part of positive psychology. As with the way of the Suffering Nation and the Suffering Servant, resurrected life comes after a dying life has been poured out for the sake of others.[12]

Within the United States Air Force is a Special Operations Unit known as the Pararescuemen (or "PJs" for short). Members train through what is known as the Pipeline: an exhaustive and exhausting program forcing applicants to defy deeply ingrained survival instincts—or fail out. This unit is one of the most broadly trained military specialists, rigorously tested for every topography and water environment, *and* equipped as a combat medic. They are "the only Department of Defense elite combat forces specifically organized, equipped, and postured to conduct full spectrum Personnel Recovery to include both conventional and unconventional combat rescue operations.

---

7   See 2 Corinthians 5:17; Colossians 2:12
8   See Hosea 3:1-3
9   Galatians 5:1
10   See Romans 6:16-20
11   See Ephesians 2:20; 4:1; Colossians 1:10; 1 Thessalonians 2:12; 1 Timothy 1:11 ('blessed' here means 'happy').
12   John 12:24

These Battlefield Airmen are the most highly trained and versatile Personnel Recovery specialists in the world."[13]

These are the men who jump out of planes and cross every imaginable terrain, not to kill or capture enemy as other Special Operations Units are assigned to do, but to extract wounded combat personnel across every branch of military and allied forces. In many ways, this is a unit of Desmond Dosses, a US Army medic who spent a night on Hacksaw Ridge during the Battle of Okinawa and pulled seventy-five wounded infantrymen off the ridge and out of certain death. The USAF Pararescuemen live and die by eight words: "The things we do, that others may live."

That others may live.

As I've learned about the Pararescuemen, I can't help but think this is the best example I've seen of the kind of laborer required to finish the Great Commission. The task will require a skill set that is both wide and deep, versatile and specific. It will require a commitment to prioritize the health and lives of others above our own. It will mean abandoning any other ambition and living in anonymity *so that others may live*. It should bother us to think men, women, and children live and die without ever receiving an opportunity to call upon the Lord and be saved.[14]

I'm not advocating for frantic evangelism. We need to prioritize prepared, equipped, skilled, versatile workers who can endure incredible stress, pressure, and violent terrain in a way we've not yet before. Some of you reading this can feel your heart racing. Maybe you need to pack your bags and hit the Pipeline.[15]

Jesus "forfeit glory to come after"[16] His dying bride, leaving behind the angelic adoration and obedience due to Him by everything He has made. He did this so that you could live. So that I could live. So that others may live. The Father adopted you at great cost to Himself and His Son so that you could live. This is the Image we are made in, the mirror recovered and cleaned up in regeneration and sanctification.

---

13   USAF. "Pararescue," (2010). Accessed July 2017. Retrieved from http://www.af.mil/About-Us/Fact-Sheets/Display/Article/104515/pararescue/.

14   See Romans 10:13-15

15   Visit faimission.org/training for more information.

16   Fraser, Brooke. (2006). "Hymn." On Albertine, audio. Columbia.

This is the holy task we're called to in the Great Commission. No honest minister or missionary enters the field for fame, fortune, or human adulation. In fact, doing so would defy the very nature of the office, which is to dutifully serve the bride as a "friend of the Bridegroom."[17] All is for His glory.[18] All is for His name, so that others may call upon it and be saved. We go so that others may live. We declare so that others may live. At the end of it all, when we've done everything we're told to do, "we are unworthy servants, who only did our duty."[19] Is His goal and glory enough for us?

Certainly, this will cost us. It will require sacrifice and suffering. If we lose sight of Jesus' worth, the Father's fame, and why we started running this race to begin with, we will become bitter and disillusioned. But if we stay the course, and serve until our sweat is mingled with blood, we will find something of our Lord and Lover of our souls—something we would not have found if we refused to mine the depths of His emotional and tangible intercession. We have an exclusive invitation to fellowship with Him in suffering[20] withheld from every other creature in the cosmos—in this age.

What will we wish we did when all is said and done, and there are no more to let live?

---

17 John 3:29
18 Gottshall, Lisa; Hackett-Park, Laura. (2011). "All is for Your Glory." On Magnificent Obsession, audio. Forerunner Music. Lyrics lean heavily on Isaiah 2:12,17.
19 Luke 17:10
20 Philippians 3:10

CHAPTER EIGHTEEN

MANIFOLD WISDOM

NINETEENTH-CENTURY PASTOR R.C. CHAPMAN once described fellowship with God in this way: "When we say, 'Lord, bring us near to Thyself,' we pray for many things, which, when they come, will be bitter to our taste. At such times it is well to remember our Forerunner: He asked to be glorified; but before heaven was opened to Him and He received therein, He had to pass through the garden of Gethsemane, and on the Cross to cry, 'My God, My God, why hast Thou forsaken Me?'"[1]

In an epic poem Scripture refers to as the "song of all songs,"[2] we follow the journey of two lovers; a king and bridegroom, and his young bride-to-be. As immutable and immortal as the Word of the LORD is, this holy tool for teaching, training, and correction by which Christ is to have preeminence,[3] we must know the fundamental illustration of a bride and bridegroom is a painted portrait of Christ and His betrothed. Pioneer missionary Hudson Taylor wrote of this book:

> *"All Scripture is given by inspiration of God and is profitable, and hence no part is, or can be, neglected without loss. Few*

---

1   Chapman, R.C. (Date unknown.) Choice sayings (being notes of expositions of the Scriptures). Marshall, Morgan & Scott Ltd.: London & Edinburgh, 32.
2   Song of Solomon 1:1
3   2 Timothy 3:16-17; Colossians 1:18

> *portions of the Word will help in the devout student more in the pursuit of this all-important 'knowledge of God' than the too-much neglected 'Song of Solomon.'*[4]

In eight chapters, we find song for so many seasons of our lives—from comfort, delight, desire, and pursuit, to cowardice, betrayal, mistreatment, and abuse (none from the hand of the king). Jesus is *the* Bridegroom, and the Shulamite's journey in this song is our own.

The writer of the epistle to the Hebrews exhorted his readers to "remove everything that entangles" us, sin which so easily ensnares, and burdens that weigh us down as we run this race of life.[5] He didn't make this up on his own. The Lord inspired those words because He wants us free of unnecessary burdens, able to run without tripping over the wires of a haphazard life. When He calls His beloved to "come away" with Him,[6] it is not so she can pack-mule fears, anxieties, and apprehensions across the hills. It is so she can be with Him where He is, where perfect love casts out every ensnaring emotion.[7] Indeed, "jealousy is a husband's fury," and He wants "all" of her.[8] He wants all of us. He wants all of you.

One of the earliest contributions to the biblical canon is the book of Job. In it, a faithful, obedient man is suddenly and heavily afflicted. To what end? His allegiances are tested. The "accuser of the brethren"[9] accused Job of being fickle, and essentially accused the Lord of stroking Job's ego for the sake of His own.[10] Job's Good Shepherd responds with expanded parameters for the enemy to sift the man.

He would later ask to do the same to Peter.[11] In all likelihood, you'll experience something to this end in your own life. Sifting is something like the Lord turning the lights off in the room you're in, and waiting for you to figure out what you believe when you can't see. It will come in many forms, produce different results, and push you to

---

4   Taylor, J. Hudson. Union and Communion: Thoughts on the Song of Solomon, (1914). FAI Publishing: Ellerslie. Kindle location 13.
5   Hebrews 12:1
6   Song of Solomon 2:10
7   John 17:24; 1 John 4:18
8   Proverbs 6:34; Deuteronomy 6:5; Matthew 22:37; Luke 10:27; Mark 12:30-31
9   Revelation 12:10
10 Job 1:6-12
11 Luke 22:31-34

different desperate ends every time. What we must know in the dark is that our Father hasn't gone anywhere and hasn't changed—but Satan will devote himself to convincing us through every dark and desperate minute that Jesus isn't there and isn't good. He'll hit you with the same Genesis 3 refrain: Can you trust Him? Did He *really* say? With any luck, he'll get you to put a gun in your mouth.[12] He is out to steal, kill, and destroy.[13] That's not a joke. Jesus didn't lay out the devil's game plan for a Sunday school rhyme. That's real life. He wants you dead. If he can't kill you, he wants you derailed and disobedient.

Why the extremity? Why sifting? Why suffering? What does this have to do with the fame of the name of the LORD? Why bother? Why would Jesus ordain this kind of thing to come into our lives?

These are all very good and very necessary questions.

When Paul wrote to the thriving and vibrant church in Ephesus about the beautiful truths of the Gospel, the inheritance of Jesus in His bride, and the magnificent calling every believer is to "walk worthy" of,[14] he began to pray for them— that this congregation that had seen revival and been taught by Timothy would be knit, both as individuals and a community, into the foundation of God's love for them, much like a tree is sustained by water to its root system. One has to wonder if this fatherly apostle saw warning signs in the culture of the community; Jesus would later rebuke them for working for Him without loving Him—for duty without beauty.[15] But as Paul began to pray for them, he stopped himself short. He had to explain some things first.

With no small amount of holy confidence, he laid out his calling before God and man: as God does with all saints, He dispensed to Paul a measure of grace to steward as a means of edifying the Body of Jesus,[16] which at that stage required the revelation of yet-hidden mysteries. He wrote, "To me, though I am the very least of all saints, this grace was given, to preach to the Gentiles the unsearchable riches

---

12 Example: Judas Iscariot.
13 John 10:10
14 Ephesians 4:1; Colossians 1:10
15 See Revelation 2:1-7
16 Ephesians 3:1-8; 4:7

of Christ, and to bring to light for everyone what is the plan of the mystery hidden for ages in God who created all things."[17]

We must pause here a moment and realize what he is saying. "God appointed me of all people to tell you all what He's up to, why He set this all up the way He did—Eden, Abraham, Jerusalem, Calvary... everything. Here's why." So you can imagine the Ephesians leaning in to listen as this letter is being read aloud at small group and such—God is letting us know what all of this is for? What would you suppose began to run through their minds? For His glory? For our salvation? For both? For the nations to know His name? For all of the above?

For Him to show off. To the devil.

"So that through the church the manifold wisdom of God might now be made known to the rulers and authorities in the heavenly places. This was according to the eternal purpose that He has realized (achieved) in Christ Jesus our Lord, in whom we have boldness and access through our faith in Him."[18]

Before we get offended at what sounds like a divine ego trip, we need to peer into this—it is a mystery, withheld from human sight for a long, long time, and must be treated as such—we should look again at what we know. We know the LORD is love. He is kind. He is compassionate. He is gracious. He doesn't excuse sin, but generously gets involved in our mud and mess to pull us out of it. He made everything we see and can't see—including meerkats on the African Sahara, and He paints sunsets only they and their zebra friends and other animals can see. He is good. So why set this whole thing up so He can show some angels and demons how wise He is?

By grace through faith in Christ, men and women are given a relationship with the Holy that is withheld even from the angelic—something into which they long to even look.[19] The Image we bear as a two-gender species reflects intimate elements of who He is they are not crafted to know, experience, or participate in. We are. Our lifelong process of shaping and forging into conformed images of the Cruciform is reserved only to us. It is between us and our Maker. No

---

17   Ephesians 3:8-9
18   Ephesians 3:11–12
19   1 Peter 1:12

one and nothing else gets to partake in this—which means we display something of Him only we can.

When we exalt Him over ourselves, something about Him is put on display for all the cosmos to see. When we turn from wicked desires or secondary pleasures and choose Him, something about Him is broadcast to the heavens. The stars shout His glory, and so do we. This universe is an orchestra of His praise, and we are central to the melody. When Job suffered for reasons unknown to him, the Voice in the whirlwind put an end to finite accusations and melodrama—and rather than receiving a backhanded smiting, Job was blessed with temporal pleasures beyond what he had before, and now knew something of his Maker he wouldn't have known otherwise. Their relationship was deeper, stronger, and yet more tender-hearted than it was before. Was it painful? Yes. Was it worth it? Absolutely.

James can thus instruct us to "count it all joy" when we encounter "various trials," knowing it produces *sufficiency* and *steadfastness* in our faith.[20] Peter, that feisty pioneer and pastor, would echo this doctrine as he celebrated the sure inheritance of the saints—to be overwhelmed with the kindness and goodness of our Father for all the ages to come[21]—and reminded us that we have something to rejoice in, even while we are grieved. *Grieved*. Rejoicing even while we suffer incredible loss. Even when we bury babies too young to die. Even when we are betrayed. Even when we are abused. Even when we lose it all. Even when "we [get] one morning with the world before us as usual, and [go] to bed that same evening completely and entirely ruined."[22] Even then, and even more.

These are not easy answers, nor are these easy waters to swim through. Life in this age can be *brutal*—in our birth nations, in our hometowns, in our native cultures. It is a challenge for many to get out of bed much of the time, without even considering a life spent under the external pressures of cross-cultural ministry. Solomon's song is only eight chapters long, and seems to skip over hardships and difficult decisions. How does anybody reach unequivocal, wholehearted surrender and trust in a Lover we cannot see with our eyes?

---

20 James 1:2

21 Ephesians 2:7

22 Murray, Ian H. *J.C. Ryle: Prepared to Stand Alone*, (2016). Carlisle, PA: The Banner of Truth Trust, p. 66.

I believe the prophets and apostles take us by the hand to illuminate in fuller explanation what it is the Shulamite saw in the King that brought her to abandon everything for Him. When Paul described the wisdom of God as "manifold," he used the same term James used to describe "various" trials. It means multi-colored, like a prism is made of dynamic nuance. Like when a diamond radiates in a hundred directions and illuminates prisms in every angle when turned in even a single beam of light. For these men, it was neither a convenient way to describe variety, nor an accidental term.

Immediately after Isaiah described the Suffering Servant in chapter 53, he turned his attention to the suffering nation bound by the Abrahamic covenant to serve as an object lesson in the nature and character of God to the rest of the nations. The implications and repercussions of this holy relationship has cost Israel everything over the years. She has been, and will always be, held to a higher standard than any other nation on the earth for all of human history—because of her irrevocable calling she did not ask for. Abraham did not ask to father a multitude that would serve the nations as an international light to whom all the earth would stream. Moses did not ask that his people bear the stewardship of the priesthood. David did not ask to guard, keep, or expand his people's territories. Hosea did not ask to marry a whore. Whatever your calling is, you didn't ask for that either. These things are assigned to us before we take our first breath.[23] We can't earn what we don't deserve. We are made by Him, through Him, and for Him, to the purposes and praise of His glory.[24]

Israel had heard a lot of promises that hadn't—and still have not—been altogether fulfilled. The prophet addresses the shame of her isolation and aborted grandeur, the bitter disappointment of forlorn dreams, and the bitter sickness of deferred hope. The LORD reminds her He is not only the Author of her days and dreams, and not only did He fashion her, but He is covenantally bound to her. He is her *Husband*, and He isn't going anywhere. Sin had fractured their relationship, and continues to now, but He *will* finish what He started. "This is like the waters of Noah to Me," He said. They rose, and then rescinded. Covenantal infidelity brought covenantal discipline, because He is faithful even when she wasn't, isn't, and even when we

---

23 Psalm 139:13–16; Jeremiah 1:5 (as an example); Ephesians 2:10
24 Ephesians 1:6,12

aren't.[25] But they did not drown the earth forever. Then He comforts her with stunning language:

> *"O you afflicted, tossed with tempest and not comforted,*[26]
>
> *Behold, I will lay your stones with colorful gems and lay your foundations with sapphires.*
>
> *I will make your pinnacles of rubies, your gates of crystal, and all your walls of precious stones."*[27]

He goes on to reiterate promises He's made before, just to make it clear He hasn't forgotten about them—not the promises, and not the people to whom He bound the integrity of His word—but before all this, He described what John the Beloved saw in his Revelation of Jesus: "the Bride, the wife of the Lamb," the "holy city Jerusalem" descending from heaven, a "city whose builder and maker is God," whose Maker is her Husband.[28] The eternal city described in Revelation 21 fits the same description written by Isaiah in his fifty-fourth chapter. We have *tremendous* courage to take from this.

Our Father of lights and glory, who dwells in unapproachable light, inhabits eternity, and whom no man has or can see, manifested Himself in the glowing face of the Son of God, Jesus of Nazareth.[29] The dusty Incarnation of the Holy was the fruition of very beautiful, very literal promises. Likewise, He really is building an actual city, and we really will live in it. But we can also be sure, anchored in His dealings with Jerusalem by this covenant every confessing Gentile is grafted into in Christ, He deals with us in the same way. He sympathizes with our afflictions in the same way—even when we're suffering the consequences of our own sin and stupidity.[30] He counts the trials of affliction when others abuse, mistreat, and betray us.[31] He sees the painful grief afflicted upon us by the deteriorating world

---

25 See 2 Timothy 2:13
26 See Isaiah 40:1
27 Isaiah 54:11-12
28 Revelation 21:9-10; Hebrews 11:10; Isaiah 54:5
29 Isaiah 57:15; John 1:18; 12:41; 2 Corinthians 4:6; Ephesians 1:17; 1 Timothy 6:16; James 1:17; 1 John 4:12
30 See Hebrews 4:15
31 See Psalm 34:19

exiled from Eden. He is present through every affliction delivered by His hand to save us from apostasy.[32] Every single one is stacked like a precious jewel, our own ebenezer of remembrance, brought by the blood of the Everlasting Covenant into the marvelous light and glory of His beautiful face, reflecting every awe and wonder through every shade known and unknown in dazzling diamonds and prisms. The multicolored wisdom of God is displayed through multicolored afflictions to the rulers and powers of the air, by the people of God who survive this age of sin and suffering for a salvation that will not disappoint us. We are not pawns on His chessboard. We are His prize, His dazzling and radiating wife, "having the glory of God"[33] through all the mind-blowing ages to come. We are His, and we will look like Him.

Scripture gives us glimpses through song and psalm and story of the mature wife of the Lamb, who is brought out of wilderness and affliction "leaning on her Beloved."[34] The life of the corporate Body, and our own as individual lovers and disciples of the Suffering Servant, has not yet reached the end of precisely numbered days. We have much to learn and reveal about Him before it does—and it will require an incarnate witness of the God Incarnate for us.

---

32   Psalm 119:71
33   Revelation 21:11
34   Song of Solomon 8:5

CHAPTER NINETEEN

Gethsemanes and Golgothas

"WE GLORY IN TRIBULATIONS, knowing that tribulation produces perseverance; and perseverance, character; and character, hope. Now hope does not disappoint, because the love of God has been poured out in our hearts by the Holy Spirit who was given to us."[1]

Paul's perspective in suffering did not come to him overnight. He lived through enough pain (physical, relational, emotional) to experience the faithfulness of God through trials to a depth and degree that forged unwavering confidence in the hope of heaven. His faith, by the time he wrote the Romans, had years of testimonies and stories undergirding it. Be encouraged by Paul's life to find Jesus working within yours.

This was not unique to Paul. Peter had grown so accustomed to trials that he bluntly instructs us to not be surprised by their presence in our lives.[2] James encouraged us not only to count suffering as "all joy," but to visit widows and orphans in their affliction—meaning, we can (and should) be so undaunted by suffering that we can serve

---
[1] Romans 5:3-5
[2] See 1 Peter 4:12

others in theirs.[3] The fires of trials are those which forge the gold of Christlikeness in us; the cold "north winds"[4] of adversity that stretch our commitment to the LORD beyond our own comforts. Jesus Himself "learned obedience by the things He suffered."[5] Our trials, our garden prayers soaked with sweaty blood, and our splintered planks of bloody wood mounted in places named for skulls are not without point and purpose. They are not orchestrated or allowed in our lives because our Father is cruel. They are orchestrated and allowed because He is using this age to craft a particular image of the Christ—the slaughtered King—into those who bear His Image; those who will rule and reign with Him forever. To those who are given much, much—more than we could know—is required.[6]

C.S. Lewis once commented that if you can experience something of the abandonment Jesus felt on the cross without getting down from it, the devil has lost you forever.[7] I am confident that we are meant to feel something of that pain, and I am confident that we are destined to not get down from our own crosses. My confidence is in this: the LORD is not out to abuse us or break us for malicious purposes. He is out to purge us of the devastating consequences that cancerous sin has wrought on our frames and souls, and turn us into something beautiful. Brands plucked from the fire. If we can hold fast to the anchor of our souls through the tumult and tempests threatening to thrash us, we lose what we can't keep and gain what we can't lose.[8]

In Jesus, our suffering has an eternal dignity. This is true for us personally, and it is true for our body of believers throughout history corporately. As we are brought into full maturity of the knowledge of Jesus, His bride will become one "made ready," a partner fit to live

---

3   James 1:2,27
4   Song of Solomon 4:16
5   Hebrews 5:8
6   Luke 12:48
7   Lewis, C.S. *The Screwtape Letters*, (1948). United Kingdom: Geoffrey Bles.
8   This is a paraphrase of the martyr Jim Elliot who said, "He is no fool who gives what he cannot keep to gain that which he cannot lose." [*Shadow of the Almighty: The Life and Testament of Jim Elliot* by Elizabeth Elliot, (1958), 108]. Though often attributed to Elliot, it is likely the quotation originated from Matthew Henry's biography of his father, English nonconformist clergyman Philip Henry (1631-1696), as "He is no fool who parts with that which he cannot keep, when he is sure to be recompensed with that which he cannot lose." [Matthew Henry, *The Life of the Rev. Philip Henry, A.M.*, Matthew Henry, ed. Sir J. B. Williams, (W. Ball, 1839), 35].

and work alongside Him.[9] We must marvel at His intention to take so many people so given to selfish ambition and bring them (us) into full maturity and complementary likeness to the Son of God.

So we must know that to "have this mind in us also" as Paul described in Philippians 2, is not a cute idea that the apostle thought might be nice. We think like Jesus or we aren't like Jesus. We will not enter the next age half-like Jesus. The Body of Jesus will match its Head.[10] If we bow the knee to a King who pinned Himself with rusty nails to splintered planks of bloody wood, we must understand life may include the same for us. Literally or figuratively, we are to pick our cross up every day and be conformed into the image of the One who loves us and gave Himself for us because we love Him and will give ourselves to Him. That is the union in glory He prayed for in John seventeen.

Jesus spent His final moments on this unrenewed earth, in this present evil age, bleeding out every drop of blood in His body. "I have manifested Your Name,"[11] He reported, and exhaled His last breath with this determined cry: "It is finished!"[12] His part and His role to secure the salvation, rescue, and deliverance of every single one given to Him from His Father was done. His assignment in this age was fulfilled. He did it. He came. He saw. He conquered. He had a task appointed to Him, and He obeyed His orders.

Our maturity in the revelation of Jesus, per the promises of Ephesians 4, will look like fully reflecting Jesus, fully serving and working alongside Him. He had a task in this age, and so do we. He was assigned with an eternally significant job, and so are we. He had orders appointed to Him, and so do we. He was ordained to pour His life out, and so are we. He was meant to glorify His Father's name, and so are we. The knowledge of God will cover the earth like the waters cover the sea.[13] We're part of that story. From sun up to sun down, the name of the LORD will be exalted in every nation.[14] We're part of that story. Obedience cost Jesus everything. Obedience will cost us everything. It was worth it for Him, it will be worth it for us.

---

9   Revelation 19:7
10   Ephesians 4:1-16
11   John 17:6
12   John 19:30
13   See Habakkuk 2:14
14   Malachi 1:11

Before His return, we'll have paid every cost, counted every lesser gain as loss, and the bride of Christ will bear her own Golgotha upon a lashed back. She'll find her victory in her own Place of the Skull, and declare triumphantly to her Father arranging the wedding of the ages: "It is finished."

Section Six

Till the Day Breaks

> *"Until the day breaks*
> *And the shadows flee away,*
> *I will go my way to the mountain of myrrh*
> *And to the hill of frankincense."*
>
> Song of Solomon 4:6

CHAPTER TWENTY

Days & Darkness

THE PROPHETS, PATRIARCHS, PSALMISTS, and apostles all pointed to and described the hour of history just before the return of the LORD. Isaiah identified the age-old "controversy of Zion,"[1] with its inception in the tents of Abraham, reaching an astonishing climax as the God of Israel avenges and vindicates the promises and provisions of the Everlasting Covenant made with Abraham. Jesus, quoting "the prophet Daniel," referred to it as the "Great Tribulation"[2] (which is the language most of us are most familiar with). Perhaps most soberly, Jeremiah delivered this decree:

> *"Thus says the LORD:*
>
> *We have heard a cry of panic, of terror, and no peace.*
>
> *Ask now, and see, can a man bear a child?*
>
> *Why then do I see every man with his hands on his stomach like a woman in labor?*
>
> *Why has every face turned pale?*

---

1 See Isaiah 34:8
2 See Matthew 24:15

> *Alas! That Day is so great there is none like it; it is a time of distress [trouble] for Jacob;*
>
> *yet he shall be saved out of it.*"[3]

Almost immediately, we ask: *Why the severity?* It is a worthy question. Jeremiah immediately answers it, but before we read his answer, I want to submit that generally speaking, we hear something like this in Scripture that, if true and literal, makes us so terribly uncomfortable that we react with unsanctified reasoning: we want to say it's never going to happen, so we make excuses that make the text irrelevant. Or we want to treat the text responsibly, but we don't want to live through this or say anyone else will, so we relegate it to history and say it's already happened. Many delusions have been considered doctrines as a result, and they almost always have to do with the "time of the end."[4] The return of Jesus is our only "blessed hope,"[5] and we are generally confused about it. Confusion concerning the return of the LORD serves nothing and no one. Let's confront the things that confuse us and get clarity. Let's bring our discomforts to Jesus, and let the Word of God[6] walk us through the Word of God.

Jesus' death on Roman crossbeams on the outskirts of a Jewish Jerusalem was a cosmically crafted means of mercy, intervening to pull us out of deadly drunken stupor. We were a lot of things, "but God" intervened[7] and made us something else. He is *making* us something else, something better and much more beautiful.

We do not always want this. What is true for us is true for national Israel because it is true of human nature. We don't always want this, national Israel doesn't always want this. Humans don't always want this. In fact, any time we *do* want to be conformed into the image of Jesus for the purposes of Jesus, it is a work of the Spirit.

Thus the intervention. The precious, intimate intervention.

"Therefore, behold, I will allure her, will bring her into the wilderness

---

3   Jeremiah 30:5-7 ESV, emphasis my own.
4   Matthew 24:21
5   Titus 2:13
6   See John 1
7   Ephesians 2:4

and speak comfort to her."[8] When the LORD confronts Jacob's unbelief, it will be into the wilderness where national Israel first met their God. How often does He do this in your own life? Have you observed the means by which He presses you to return to "the love you did at first" when your affection for Him cools and allegiance wavers?[9] He is so gentle—even in severity.

National Israel will be "hedged in" with "thorns of nations"[10] because all of national Israel will have their "come to Jesus" moment—and they will, in fact, come to Jesus. They'll all see Him. They'll all see the One they pierced and will grieve the decisions they've made.[11] They'll all experience the tangible mercy and goodness of Jesus when they realize He did not return to discipline them, but to defend them. It won't be because they *deserve* to be defended. It will be because He *made them His to defend*.

The time of Jacob's trouble and return of the LORD get significant airtime throughout the Scriptures—something like 150 chapters, which is more than any other topic in the Word. Ignoring the theme is a costly offense endangering us of forewarned arrogance.[12] Throughout the book of Daniel and the Olivet discourse in particular, Jesus outlines unnerving calamities and provides explicit details Paul would later expound upon. False witnesses. Deception. Wars. Conflicts. Famines. Plagues and health crises. Earthquakes in places that normally never experience them. "All these are the beginning of sorrows."[13] The beginning of birth pangs.

"For we know the whole creation groans and labors with birth pangs until now."[14] "A woman, when she is in labor, has sorrow because her hour has come; but as soon as she has given birth to the child, she no longer remembers the anguish, for joy that a human being has been born into the world. Therefore you now have sorrow; but I will see

---

8   Hosea 2:14, NKJV
9   See Revelation 2:4
10 Hosea 2:6; Zechariah 12:2-3
11 See Zechariah 12:10; 14:4; Matthew 23:39
12 See Romans 11:25
13 Matthew 24:8 NKJV
14 Romans 8:22 NKJV

you again and your heart will rejoice, and your joy no one will take from you."[15]

Jeremiah injects this troublesome passage with this abiding hope: "And it shall come to pass in that Day, declares the LORD, that I will break his yoke from off your neck, and I will burst your bonds, and foreigners shall no more make a servant of him. But they shall serve the LORD their God and David their king, whom I will raise up for them."[16]

We have seen and heard no shortage of sensationalism swirling around the biblical texts concerning the end of the age and return of Jesus. It's made many level-headed people afraid of coming near the issue, let alone speaking about it publicly, and we're missing out on more than milk as a result. Many would object they just want to love Jesus and not worry about eschatology and end-times conjecture. I humbly submit this: the last word given in the Scriptures is the most detailed and dedicated commentary on eschatological dynamics, it is specifically referred to as "the revelation of Jesus Christ," and even John the Beloved hardly recognized the Man when he saw Him.[17] The return of our Lord and Savior is a Christological issue and nothing less. We must view and treat it appropriately, and we should anticipate it with hope in our hearts for the restoration of all things, knowing it brings the people of the covenant back into unwavering covenantal fidelity.

This age gives birth to the next when the LORD returns. This is about us being with Jesus forever. This is about Israel no longer resisting or refusing the reign of David's Son. No prophet, patriarch, psalmist, or apostle wrote about the days and darkness prior to the LORD's return because they *wanted* to see calamity befall humanity. They wrote about it because the Spirit of the LORD gripped their hearts to *want* the restoration of all things, and they shared what He revealed to prepare us for it.

It is not simply a better hope. It is a *blessed* hope.

---

15   John 16:21-22 NKJV
16   Jeremiah 30:8-9
17   See Revelation 1:1,12-17

CHAPTER TWENTY-ONE

MADE AND ALLOWED TO UNDERSTAND

NO PROPHET SAW THE DAY OF THE LORD and slept easily that night. We cannot expect to do the same. We also cannot avoid scriptural topics and themes simply because they make us uncomfortable, and we cannot feign ignorance over something so pervasive throughout the biblical texts. The Day of the LORD, the return of Jesus, and the inauguration of the Son of David's kingdom is by far and away the most repeated, discussed, and thoroughly addressed issue between Genesis and Revelation. I believe we were given the holy canon because our Father is a good shepherd who will not leave us unprepared for the days ahead.

We have been traumatized by apocalyptic sensationalism and disobedient date-setting. However, no trauma is an excuse to willfully ignore the revelation of Jesus Christ now and at the end of the age. It is personally and pastorally irresponsible to disregard the prophetic literature, testimony of the prophets, promise to the patriarchs, and purpose behind the apostolic ministry. The King is coming. We are "children of the light"[1] and not darkness. We have the Helper with us and the written texts before us. We are therefore without excuse

---

1   See 1 Thessalonians 5:4-6

to give less than due diligence to the instruction of the Word of the LORD.

"When you see the abomination of desolation spoken of by the prophet Daniel, standing in the holy place (let the reader understand), then let those who are in Judea flee to the mountains."[2] Jesus' injection of a four-word parenthetical phrase is both a command and His determined intercession for our own good and growth. *Let the reader understand.* He is emphasizing our need to do our homework, and read the words written by the prophet Daniel (as well as emphasizing the simple fact that the book of Daniel was written by one man: a prophet named Daniel, knowing liberal scholarship would contest this later). He's contending on our behalves, that we would receive the understanding Daniel himself received—removing any question or doubt that He wants us to understand this, and will help us do so.

It is common within Christian vernacular to use the term "Daniel fast." Generally we're referring to a three-week period during which we abstain from "meats and sweets," forgoing steaks and chocolate and devoting time and energy to the Word in a particular way. What might be less common is the knowledge that the three-week model we're leaning on was when Daniel, already decades into a lifestyle of fasting, saw the time of Jacob's trouble and begged heaven for understanding.

It was given to him.

This should encourage us. Yet revelation did not come without resistance,[3] and this should sober us.

An angel named Gabriel is identified in three conversations with humans throughout Scripture: Zacharias (the father of John the Baptist), Mary (the mother of Jesus), and Daniel. Of all the angelic encounters recorded in the canon,[4] of all the assignments angels were dispatched to execute, only three times are we confident Gabriel was the one present. Once on the Day of Atonement,[5] to tell the highest ranking priest within Israel that he and his wife's aged bodies would bear a similar testimony to Abraham and Sarah; to bear an unlikely son who would serve a greater purpose than they could

---

[2] Matthew 24:15-16, ESV
[3] See Daniel 10:2-3; 12-14
[4] "The biblical canon" refers to the sixty-six books of the Bible.
[5] See Daniel 9 and Luke 1

fathom—preparing the nation of the covenant for the first appearance of the Son of the everlasting covenant. Another to tell a young girl in the middle of her engagement that she would become pregnant with the holy Son who would bleed for the covenant. Before all this, he fought off the principality ruling the atmosphere over Persia to find Daniel, and help him understand his visions of the context before and during the coming of the Son of Man, who would vindicate and fulfill the covenant.

Gabriel's message to Daniel was no less important than his messages to Zechariah and Mary. We cannot escape the centrality of the covenant in Scripture, and we cannot "understand" if we do not give the issue due honor as assigned by the LORD in His Word. It is so pervasive throughout the text, that eschatological ignorance can only reflect biblical illiteracy. Jesus' command to "let the reader understand" essentially meant "get in the Word." As angels to Ezekiel, Jeremiah, and John put it, "eat the scroll."[6] It is only by the same prayer, fasting, and humility wrought within Daniel that we can saturate in Scripture and receive revelation by the merciful hand of our generous Father who does not mock us when we admit our need for wisdom.[7]

"Understanding" the times and seasons, and "understanding" the Word of the LORD does not mean we master the text and check a passing score off our list of things to achieve. It means we have bowed our minds below the authority of the Scriptures, rather than elevating our cognitive prowess over it, as though the Bible were some kind of college dissertation we're meant to dissect and exert judgment over. If we are not burdened to pursue knowledge, if we do not ask for the wisdom we've been guaranteed, and if we trip over our own ego and fall short of humble prayer and fasting as we seek Jesus, we deserve the ignorance presently cloaking the issue of the covenant and the end in general conversation and convictions throughout the western Church. It is certainly not Jesus' fault that we're in the dark, and drunkenly tolerating less than cunning fables in evangelical media endeavors. He's given us everything we need for life and godliness,[8] and summons our attention every time we open His Word.

Let's get in the Word.

---

6   See Ezekiel 3:1-3; Jeremiah 15:16; Revelation 10:9-10
7   James 1:5-7; 16-17
8   See 2 Peter 1:3

CHAPTER TWENTY-TWO

Watching Weather

IN MATTHEW 16, THE LEADERS OF THE JEWISH COMMU-NITY approached Jesus and asked Him to provide some kind of sign to confirm whether or not He was the Messiah. If the promised One stood before them, it meant everything for their hour of history and would change so much of how they would respond, teach, and lead their communities as teachers and shepherds. They wanted to be sure before they made such a gamble. Fair enough, right?

Jesus immediately condemned them for asking. He called them "wicked" and "adulterous"[1]—it would have been difficult for Him to use stronger language, or choose more loaded terms. They weren't accusations. They were statements. If Jesus calls you wicked and adulterous, you check yourself before you wreck yourself. Why would He have responded to their curiosity with such condemnation?

Wickedness is opposition to the Holy One. It is a perversion of order, deviance from His design, and defiance of His intentions. Adultery is the grotesque fruit of a heart that gives what was committed to a covenantal partner away to swine instead. Their affections were mixed and their allegiances muddied. If they *hadn't* opposed Him, but instead walked in humble submission, they would have received a different response. If they hadn't given themselves away to the pride of life and

---

[1] Matthew 16:4

the lusts of the flesh, He would have celebrated and affirmed their fidelity. Simeon and Anna both recognized their Messiah while He was still in diapers.[2] Why couldn't these men identify Him as a grown man?

We do not need signs when we have explicit Scriptures. It is true and fair to honor that their hearts were hardened in unbelief.[3] It is also true and fair to honor what the LORD will reveal to those who come to Him in contrition.[4] Here is what we must learn from their exchange with Jesus and ask our Helper to examine us regarding: do we trust the integrity of His Word? Is it sufficient for us? Do we love His Scriptures? Or must we beg for further signs?

The LORD knows our hearts, and sees everything.[5] There's a profound difference between arrogance and immaturity—*and*, all healthy things grow. Our good Father wants us to grow us.[6]

"A wicked and adulterous generation seeks after a sign, and no sign shall be given to it except the sign of the prophet Jonah." The sign of the man who spent three days in the belly of a whale on a mission to preach mercy to Gentiles alienated from the covenant.[7] "I'm about to pull an Ephesians 2:11-22. That's what you'll see, and that's all you're going to see." There is a storyline threaded throughout the canon of Scripture, and it is not difficult to identify. This "present evil age"[8] is cloaked in darkness, and the sun is dawning on the horizon. The knowledge of the glory of the LORD will cover the earth as the waters cover the seas. This is about Him; His fame, His Name; His glory. Can we see the rising sun?

Jesus' response to the teachers of His time implies He is confident we already have all the information we need. "When it is evening you say, 'It'll be fair weather, for the sky is red,' and in the morning you say, 'It'll be foul weather, for the sky is red and threatening.' Hypocrites! You know how to discern the face of the sky, but you cannot discern

---

2   See Luke 2:21-38
3   Romans 1:18-32
4   See Isaiah 66:1-2
5   See 2 Chronicles 16:9; Proverbs 5:21; Isaiah 66:2; Hebrews 4:13
6   See 1 Corinthians 3:2; Hebrews 5:12-14
7   A process that would, invariably, harden Israel's heart against the LORD. See Romans 9-11, and *KING OF SHADOWS 04 // The Prophet and the Sea* by FAI STUDIOS, 2018.
8   Galatians 1:4

the signs of the times." Imagine having dinner with your family on your balcony. If you saw a dynamic sunset in the sky at night, you would admire it. If you woke up the next morning and saw the same sky during breakfast, it would concern you. It would *alarm* you. We know when certain things should occur. Here is Jesus' confidence in what He has equipped us with: If we can tell the difference between a sunset and a coming storm, we have enough discernment to recognize what He is doing in the earth. It's that simple. So we can watch the weather with confidence that He is willing and able to guard and save us from confusion—if we are given to the Word in humble submission with prayer and fasting.

There's a peak in the Blue Ridge mountains of Georgia called Currahee, Cherokee for "stand alone." It was adopted as a motto by Easy Company of the 506th Infantry Division of the 101st Airborne during World War II, as Easy's first commanding officer employed the mountain to train the men under grueling conditions. Three miles up and three miles down, Easy had to run Currahee at any time with little to no notice, often with full packs. It prepared them for the war ahead. There's a scene in the first episode of the television series *Band of Brothers*[9] (about Easy's preparation for and work during the war, taken from accounts of surviving members of the company) in which one man had to run Currahee alone within a short time window. If he failed, he was out of the company. As he is on his way to the top, winded for breath and driven by the fear of losing his place, he is joined by a handful of his buddies who volunteered to come alongside him and run Currahee with him. It was the push he needed, and he went to bed that night in the Easy Company barracks.

We stand alone together. Discipleship and obedience to Jesus is a race we all must run. As Paul put it, each has a load to carry—and burdens to bear.[10] It is appropriate to carry your own load. It is Gospel law to bear your brother's burden. We have to be willing to come alongside each other and help each other reach the top of Currahee. Sometimes, this means confronting each other's confusions and lovingly correcting each other's errors. This is precisely what George Müller was willing to do for A.T. Pierson; the latter adhered to a pre-tribulation

---

9   HBO, *Band of Brothers* (2001). Directed by Steven Spielberg. Produced by Tom Hanks. Currahee.
10 Galatians 6:2

rapture and taught this position from his pulpit. Once while traveling together, Müller leaned in with these words in response to Pierson's supporting points for his conviction: "My beloved brother, not one of them is based upon the word of God."[11]

He knew his brother's convictions were misled, misguided, and dangerous for the people entrusted by Jesus to Pierson's pastoral leadership. Are we willing to lean into our family members and tell them their confusion is neither cute nor biblical? Do we have the clarity to inform them where their convictions became misled? Müller's gracious, firm, and gentle rebuke pushed his brother into the Scriptures, into prayer, and into humility before the Author of the holy writ. Pierson emerged from the wrestle in repentance, forsaking pre-tribulation dispensationalism and embraced the post-tribulation appearance of Jesus expressed by the prophets and apostles. He later covered the pulpit of their dear friend Charles Haddon Spurgeon during the sickness that led to his death, and for considerable time afterward. He is considered one of the foremost fathers of the Student Volunteer Movement for Foreign Missions, a watershed moment for global missions in the nineteenth century.

"Concerning the times and the seasons, brethren, you have no need that I should write to you. For you yourselves know perfectly that the Day of the LORD so comes as a thief in the night." said Paul to the Thessalonians (he spent three weeks ministering to them. Consider the priority he placed upon the coming of the LORD in his crash course into Christianity teaching series).[12] He continued:

> *"For when they say, 'Peace and safety!' then sudden destruction comes upon them, as labor pains upon a pregnant woman. And they shall not escape. But you, brethren, are not in darkness, so that this Day should overtake you as a thief. You are all sons of light and sons of the day. We are not of the night nor of darkness. Therefore let us not sleep, as others do, but let us watch and be sober. For those who sleep, sleep at night, and those who get drunk are drunk at night. But let us*

---

11 Robert, Dana L. *Occupy till I Come: A.T. Pierson and the Evangelization of the World*, (2003). Wm. B. Eerdmands Publishing. Kindle location 1400.
12 Acts 17:1-2; 1 Thessalonians 5:1-8

who are of the day be sober, putting on the breastplate of faith and love, and as a helmet the hope of salvation."[13]

Does the Body of Messiah at large exhibit confidence and clarity concerning the coming of the Son of Man? I do not believe we do. Why not? We can tell the difference between a sunset and a coming storm, can we not? *We are not in darkness.* We are children of our Father of glory who dwells in unapproachable light. He doesn't do anything without first telling His servants His plans, even if He wraps them in mystery yet to be revealed. Daniel's record of the mysteries shown to him were for "the time of the end."[14] If we ask our Father for wisdom and clarity and insight, He will not leave us to our folly. When we ask Him for bread, He does not give us a stone.[15]

When watchmen were placed on the walls of Jerusalem, they did not wonder if morning would ever come. They knew they were not consigned to perpetual darkness. They knew they were assigned to a normal eight-hour shift while the city slept. So it is with this age. We know we are not consigned to perpetual darkness. We know sin and iniquity will meet their end and our bodies will be raised with the same power and to the same glory as our Lord's body was pulled out of the grave.[16] We know Jesus will return to inherit all He's been promised and all we can offer Him. So we wait for Him "more than watchmen wait for the morning."[17]

---

13 1 Thessalonians 5:1-8, emphasis my own
14 Daniel 8:17,19; 11:35,40; 12:1,4,9
15 See Matthew 7:9
16 See 1 Corinthians 15:20-23
17 Psalm 130:6

CHAPTER TWENTY-THREE

Our Blessed Hope

WHEN THE LORD PAINTS THE SCOPE AND LANDSCAPE of the future ages for us, He does not set a low vision: weeks and millennia untold without war.[1] Bodies that can't ache and hearts that are eternally immune to pain.[2] Every Jesus-loving decision will be rewarded.[3] All actions, noble and otherwise, will be recompensed. No blasphemous debt will go unsettled. Coffins will be splintered by the resurrected saints.[4] Our days will be spent basking in the light of His face and kindness, such that shame the sun.[5] These are His terms for justice and restoration; they are not vague, they cannot disappoint, and per the parameters of Scripture, we are never to lower our gaze.

It is right, then, that Paul refers to the promised return of Jesus as our "'blessed' hope."[6] His coming is the "glorious appearing of our great God and Savior,"[7] wherein the eternal balm of Gilead[8] provides sufficient salve to the wounds of this world. "Hope," wrote the apostle,

---

1 See Isaiah 2:2-4; Micah 4:1-5
2 Revelation 21:3
3 1 Corinthians 3:14; Hebrews 11:6; 2 John 1:8; Revelation 22:12
4 See 1 Corinthians 15:20-23; 1 Thessalonians 4:13-17
5 See Isaiah 24:23; 60:19-23; Revelation 21:23
6 Titus 2:13
7 Ibid.
8 Jeremiah 8:22; 46:11

is the fruit of perseverance-wrought character in trial and tribulation, and this sweet fruit of peril "does not disappoint."[9]

Jesus will not disappoint.

The Light of the world will shed revelation on all we now see but "dimly,"[10] eliminating the confusion we feel about Scriptural tensions without reducing our wonder at who He is. For now, we must read difficult, challenging, or offensive passages with the same reverence with which we read the rest. As an example, we're all comfortable with the Jesus of Isaiah 53: He who bore our griefs, carried our sorrows, received wounds for our transgressions and bruises for our iniquities, the offering and intercession for us sinners. He died our death so we could live His life. That's Gospel. That's Good News. We love that.

Ten chapters later, the same prophet describes the same Man stained with the blood of the nations as He exacts judgment during the time of trouble just before His appearing.[11] He is the slain Lamb in the center of heaven's court opening the holy scroll—"earth's title deed"[12]—one difficult seal at a time.[13] And He is the only One who can be trusted to do so because He is the slain and risen Lamb; meek enough to offer His life, humble enough to count it a privilege, and strong enough to finish what He started. That's also Good News. We must repent of the thing in us, as a collective and corporate Body of Messiah, that has scorned, rejected, mocked, ignored, or attempted to rewrite the implications of a passage like Zechariah 12, describing the LORD intentionally gathering Israel's neighbors into war against her so that He can confront them in the flesh.[14] Two chapters later,[15] Zechariah wrote that Jesus will split the Mount of Olives in two as He rescues His people from their oppressors at the end of this age—an appearance in sync with Jesus' conditional prophecy in Matthew 23: "Jerusalem, you will not see Me again until you say, 'Blessed is He who comes in

---

9   Romans 5:1-5
10 1 Corinthians 13:12
11 Isaiah 63:1-6
12 I borrow this term from Mike Bickle, who explains it at better length here: https://ihop-kcorg-a.akamaihd.net/platform/IHOP/1021/71/20141010_Jesus_Received_as_King_by_All_Nations_Rev.5.12_TMHE05_study_notes.pdf
13 See Revelation 6:1-8:5
14 See Zechariah 12:1-14
15 See Zechariah 14:1-9

the name of the LORD!'"[16] This is the same prophet who, just a few breaths before, wrote that the Son of David would come to Zion on a donkey.[17] He very literally did.[18] So when that prophet describes the calamity and close of this era of redemptive history with violent details of the LORD's intentions, we have no reason to believe He will deviate from the plan. He, very literally, will split the Mount of Olives just like He very literally rode into Zion on a donkey—to be spit on, slapped, shredded, and slaughtered. The hermeneutic (method of interpreting the text) does not change from chapter-to-chapter. We can trust the Jesus of Zechariah 12 and 14 because we trust the Jesus of Zechariah 9. When He does split the sky—with all the fire and brimstone Paul described to the Thessalonians—He will likely defy untold ideas we hold about who He is and what He's up to. One thing He will *not* do is behave inconsistently with the testimony of the Word or portray anything incongruent with Scripture.

Eden's insufficiency exposed our innately rebellious will; our flesh-borne attraction to the lures and counterfeits of idolatry and treason. "The restoration of all things"[19] will see a resurrected "bride made ready,"[20] wrought by persevering love and a regenerated, sanctified will submitted to King Jesus. Our allegiances and loyalties will be fully His, much like the crowns we will wear as rewards, yet gladly offer at His feet.[21] We will see Him, hear His decrees, and inform our days and decisions with the satisfaction we'll have in His leadership over the earth. He'll bestow upon us crowns, jewels, governance and rewards for our obedience and stewardship now, and we will very happily lay it all back before Him. It'll be humanity's healthiest, most thriving hour yet, and there are ages upon ages ahead of us.

We have much to look forward to.[22]

---

16 See Matthew 23:39
17 See Zechariah 9:9
18 See Matthew 21:2-7; John 12:14-15
19 Acts 3:21
20 Revelation 19:7
21 See Revelation 4:10
22 "There are far, far better things ahead than what we leave behind." Lewis, C.S. *Letters to an American Lady*, (1967). Eerdmans.

CHAPTER TWENTY-FOUR

Something Like Jasper

"*WHEN I SAW HIM, I FELL AT HIS FEET AS THOUGH DEAD.*"[1] It was a few decades since John the Beloved last saw Jesus in the flesh, and he hardly recognized the Man who stood before him. A political exile on a Mediterranean island, it had been a while since John had seen anyone, but this was different. This was "the revelation of Jesus Christ."[2] (If we were to wander down the rabbit hole of theological debate, we'd examine all the ways people excuse away loaded texts and castrate the promises of God in prophecy. This age ends with the return of Jesus and the resurrection of the saints. That's how we're going to read John's revelation.)

Scripture begins with setting the first Adam in a garden with his bride, and ends with the second Adam in a garden with his bride. It's important to read the texts in-between with these bookends in mind. Daniel declared we would know our waiting is over when we see the Son of Man "coming in power on the clouds of heaven," having endured through the worst trial for these good purposes: "to finish the transgression, to make an end of sins, to make reconciliation for iniquity, to bring in everlasting righteousness, to seal up vision and prophecy, and to anoint the Most Holy."[3] When the Son of Man

1 Revelation 1:17
2 Revelation 1:1
3 Daniel 9:24, NKJV

appears, every saint asleep in Christ will be plucked out of graves and caught up to meet Him in the sky[4]—and this is the end of our struggle against sin, powers, and principalities. David's Son will devote an entire age to making every wrong thing right, beginning with this: He will no longer be blasphemed, and we will no longer be covered in mud. Our filthy mirrors will be washed forever and we will "shine like the kingdom of our Father."[5]

These aren't just beautiful words. When John saw Jesus and was given a series of visions explaining how all this would take place, he first received seven letters to seven churches. We've much to glean from these still. Then John's experience continued and he saw an open door into heaven. Consider the implication here. He heard a voice, loud and confident like a trumpet: "Come up here! I will show you what must take place after this."[6] Consider the invitation here. The last book of the Bible expounds on all Daniel wrote. (Some would say we can ignore both men's writings, because they're somehow already fulfilled and relegated to the dusty shelves of history. I would say no one is resurrected yet and everyone keeps sinning, so let's not castrate the Good News of the coming Kingdom.) Just as every prophet struggled for words to communicate what they saw, John groped for language: everything was "something like" and had the "appearance of" something else for which we already have a cognitive concept. He stood on a sea of glass that was "like crystal."[7] He saw four creatures (with the interesting descriptive "living creatures") "like" an ox, "like" a lion, one that looked something "like" a man, and another "like" an eagle in flight.[8] Amazingly, "in the Spirit," he saw the One on the throne, and He looked "something like jasper."[9]

This is important language to remember, because it crops up again before the last "amen."[10]

Paul's letter to the Ephesians reminds us that the "hope to which [we are] called" is this: the "riches of [Jesus'] glorious inheritance in the

---

4   See 1 Corinthians 15:20-23; 1 Thessalonians 4:13-17
5   Matthew 13:43
6   Revelation 4:1
7   Revelation 4:6
8   Revelation 4:7
9   Revelation 4:2-3, NKJV
10 Revelation 22:21

saints."[11] By the gruesome cross, we get Him and He gets us. There is nearly no better news. For all that is due the Davidic King, we are His inheritance. If the first man in the first garden was a "type of Him who was to come,"[12] so the first woman in the first garden was a type and shadow of her own; Eve is us. We are the bride He dove six feet into the grave to ransom and redeem, successful in every way the first Adam couldn't be. We are, then, "bone of His bone, flesh of His flesh,"[13] and He will come to collect us.[14] When He does, we will look like Him. In fact, we must.

What God is doing in this age through Jerusalem, He illustrates in the lives of the saints; and vice versa. What God is doing in this age through the saints, He is illustrating in Jerusalem. When we read we are "living stones,"[15] living temples of the indwelling Holy Spirit— the "guarantee" of the coming inheritance[16]—it is not that He has abandoned His purposes for His city. He cannot do so without making Himself a liar. Conversely, when we read He will establish the storm-tossed and afflicted Jerusalem with beautiful stones,[17] we can be confident He will do the same with our testimonies and endurance. Through the interceding work of Messiah, we are identified with His city. This is what we're grafted into: Abraham's dream of a better city, and a better King.[18] The patriarch of this resurrection faith "saw Jesus' day," when sorrow, pain, and mourning ceases, when our Father wipes our tears away from our swollen eyes, when death is turned over once and for all, and he rejoiced.[19]

In that day, when Jerusalem is called "the LORD our righteousness,"[20] she will not be known for intifadas or border fences, nor checkpoints or the wailing sounds at the Western Wall. She will not be known for striving, nor knowledge that does not save. She will not be known for orthodoxy, nor will we know her by her infidelity. She will be known,

---

11 Ephesians 1:18
12 Romans 5:14
13 My paraphrase for this application of Genesis 2:23
14 1 Thessalonians 4:13-17
15 1 Peter 2:5
16 Ephesians 1:14
17 See Isaiah 54:11-17
18 See John 8:56; Hebrews 11:10
19 See John 8:56; Revelation 21:3
20 See Jeremiah 23:6; 33:16

quite simply, for the holiness of her Husband given to her by virtue of covenantal election. In the same way, we will not be known for our own blasphemies or stupid mistakes. We will not be known for our sins. We will not be seen by our stains. We will be dressed in the same white robes given to Joshua in Zechariah's vision, and we will stand on that glassy sea, white as the snow-bright hair on Jesus' head.[21] We will look like Him.

An angel tugged on John's arm: "Come, let me show you the Bride, the wife of the Lamb."[22] Reading his description, I have to wonder if John ever stopped breathing when he saw her. "The holy city" came "down from heaven" adorned "as a bride prepared for her husband," "having the glory of God," with "radiance like a most rare jewel"[23]— in fact, she looked like the One John just saw sitting on the throne. She looked "something like jasper."[24] In other words, John saw her and said:

"She looks like her Husband. She looks like her Father."

This is Jerusalem's destiny, and thus it is our own. She will not bear His Name in vain, and neither will we. Our testimonies will not be that we tried hard enough or took sufficient baths to scrub our sin away, but simply that we trusted in the God who saves and resurrects and, like the sons of Seth so long ago, "called upon the Name of the LORD."[25]

And it was enough.

---

21 See Revelation 1:14
22 Revelation 21:9
23 See Revelation 21:2,9-11
24 Revelation 21:11
25 Genesis 4:26

SECTION SEVEN

AND THE SHADOWS FLEE

"I have sometimes seen, in the morning sun, the smoke of a thousand villages where no missionary has ever been."

ROBERT MOFFAT, PIONEER TO AFRICA

CHAPTER TWENTY-FIVE

Occupy Till I Come

PAUL'S EXHORTATION TO ENDURE SUFFERING, knowing it ultimately produces hope, is not an isolated incident in Scripture; but it is perhaps the most concise principle binding the long-suffering of the saints to the long-suffering of the Lord.[1] Jesus similarly encouraged us that by patience we possess our souls, resting in great confidence in the good and qualified leadership of our Father,[2] especially regarding the timing of events He has put in His own authority—despite how desperately we may want them to happen today, or even yesterday. This cursed creation will certainly groan before His return, and we who know His name are not exempt from the strain.[3]

Regarded by many as the father of the Student Volunteer Movement for Foreign Missions (SVM), Arthur Tappan Pierson was a domestic pastor based in Detroit for much of his ministry. His philosophy and theology of ministry, work, and missions was forever shaped and altered by Mueller's rebuke of his original postmillennialism, pushing him to the parable of the nobleman and his servant's use of his money.[4] It is fairly referred to as a principle of stewardship, but it serves the text an injustice if we don't recognize that it was delivered because the

---
1 Romans 5:1-5
2 Luke 12:32; 21:19
3 Matthew 24:9; Romans 8:22
4 Luke 19:11-27

143

disciples were wondering if they were living in the Day when the Son of David would take His throne in Jerusalem.[5] Jesus told this story to emphasize diligent, responsible, God-honoring stewardship when it feels like you've been working and waiting so long for an end that may never come. In this tale, a nobleman left his land to "receive a kingdom," and instructed his servants to simply "do business until" he came back. Some invested. One ignored. It is clear from the story who we *don't* want to be.

Their imperative is our imperative. Do business until the Lord returns. Pierson's translation reads "*occupy* till I come," and it framed his watchword over the SVM: the evangelization of the whole world in their generation. Domestic ministry amongst the urban poor in Detroit was not held in competition with foreign work amongst the unreached and unengaged, but rather in conjunction with it. The Lord never released Pierson from his domestic post, but still used this American pastor to recruit new laborers, mobilize them to the field, and sustain them with vision and prayer from an ocean away. America's pulpits need more Piersons in our own day.

Two thousand years after the Lord's resurrection, ascension, and delivery of our "great commission," it is easy to slip into the kind of "business-as-usual" that numbs our hearts and dulls our vision of His soon return. Two thousand years and counting doesn't *feel* "soon."[6] It feels unlikely. We may feel discouraged. Sometimes, when our highways are filled with funeral processions and our headlines with deadly geopolitics, we feel forgotten.

"Blessed is he who believes without seeing,"[7] and can hold fast to the surety of God's promises bound to the integrity of His word. We are not without hope. We are not without destiny. We will *all* stand before our Maker and give account for our days, our decisions, and even the idle words we let escape our lips.[8] Like the servants in the story, we will all see our Master again and report what we did with what we were given in the time we were given to use the resources. He will have something to say about *all* our work. It is so important that we take our jobs seriously. Every saved saint has been made for

---

5   Luke 19:11
6   Revelation 22:20
7   John 20:29
8   See Matthew 12:36

"good works" as sure as our salvation; we've all been called to something of which we must "walk worthy."[9]

The difference between "eat, drink, and be merry, for tomorrow we die"[10] and "doing business until" our Master returns is simply whether or not we are expecting His return. Are we living in light of eternity, or are we living for tomorrow? Are our minds set on things above, hands set on the plow assigned to us, and eyes set on the joy set before us?[11] Or are we simply surviving and getting by? It is not a fear of failure that keeps me up at night. It is a fear of wasting time.[12]

In a letter to Timothy, Paul reminded him that no good soldier gets entangled in civilian affairs.[13] We have been trained for tasks and assigned to posts. If you're not clear about what yours is, press into prayer with your Potter and ask Him what shapes the clay of your life is meant to take. As you do so, simply look around. Where are you? "To him who is faithful, more will be given."[14] Do not seek satisfaction in "more" when you've despised what you've already been given. Prove yourself with what you've already been entrusted with. The Lord called me to serve Him at a certain Starbucks store while I was in university before He ever called me to a new nation. All my co-workers received a witness of Jesus, and many hadn't before. I had to learn to love bothersome college roommates before He entrusted me with the messy glory that is a pioneering team on the frontier, and I made a lot of lattes before I ever made a film.

Let us not be deluded to believe ministry in any expression will save us from the diligent task of seeking the Lord daily. God and life will escort us into seasons of excitement and enthralling joy when we read our Bibles. God and life will also escort us into seasons of impossible boredom, prodding us to wonder what we are satisfied by—circumstances or the unchanging character of our Father in heaven. Days will come when you think you've done it all, heard it all, seen it all, and there's nothing new under the sun.[15] Seek and serve Jesus then.

---

9   Ephesians 4:1; Colossians 1:10; 1 Thessalonians 2:12
10 Ecclesiastes 8:15; Luke 12:19
11 See Luke 9:62; Colossians 3:1-2; Hebrews 12:2
12 Or, as William Carey (pioneer missionary to India) put it, "I am not afraid of failure. I am afraid of succeeding at things that do not matter."
13 See 2 Timothy 2:3
14 Matthew 13:12; 25:29; Mark 4:24-25; Luke 8:18; 12:48
15 See Ecclesiastes 1:9

Others will arrive in the morning, and remind you before bedtime that you don't know anything. Lean on Jesus on those days. Days will come when you think you've read all the verses, sung all the songs, and prayed all the prayers. Seek and serve Jesus on those days too. Others will wake you up and startle you, surprise you, or sabotage you. Lean on Jesus those days especially, knowing His Day is coming soon.

As I write this, I am a single woman in my early thirties with a passport book running out of room for stamps. Name a continent; I've probably been on it. Name an ocean; I've likely swum in it. If I had a dollar for every time someone whose life doesn't often put them on an airplane has told me my life is so "exciting," I would not need to raise support anymore. I'd be a fully-funded missionary. Here is what I know: I've woken up in a small town in the Midwestern plains, and I've woken up in a mountain valley town in the Middle East (often due to Turkish jets flying low where they don't belong, or the Islamic call to prayer before daybreak—and who can sleep at all during Ramadan?). I have been bored out of my mind in both locations, and particularly beautiful ones. Nothing has frustrated me more than hiking up an extinct volcano to watch the sun set over the South Pacific, and realizing the stunning beauty of created order did nothing to satiate what is ultimately a craving for Jesus. If we are not satisfied in Him, we will not be satisfied by an assignment in Iowa, Istanbul, or anywhere in-between.

"'Doing business' until the Lord returns" means being faithful with what you've been given, and responding to pruning and promotion with consistent reliance on His good leadership over your life. I've spent some years now in 'prayer and missions movements,' and have heard enough stream-specific language to fill another book (I'll spare you here). What is important to point out is that even in these communities so committed to things that very clearly take time—lifelong habits of days spent in prayer and the Word, the laborious task of finding the last person to hear about Jesus (and learning their foreign language to deliver the glorious message)—I've still heard way too much sensational rhetoric, and seen way too many runners drop out of the race because they're bitterly disappointed with how difficult it proves to be. Our American mentality of 'get your cold food hot in a minute' gets railed on, but telling young adults to 'fast and pray through their twenties so they can walk in power in their thirties' is one semantic side of the same narrow-minded coin. Adding a decade to the microwave and hoping for the best usually leads to disillusionment. It leads faithful people to believe they're "doing it wrong." We often create what we believe are biblical principles, brow-beat with a man-made 'word of the Lord,' and then get confused when Jesus doesn't respond to us gamblers like some kind of rigged slot machine. It's a dangerous expectation to see a ten-year turnaround from the God who made Moses spend eighty in the desert. Drink no Kool-Aid that will cause you to despise the "waste" of a life of obedience.[16]

We bow to the God of Abraham, Isaac, and Jacob. He cannot be predicted. He cannot be coerced. He cannot be manipulated. Do business till He comes back, and be faithful to your very big, very mysterious Lord. That's what the world needs from you.

---

16 Matthew 26:8; Mark 14:4

CHAPTER TWENTY-SIX

Work that Survives Fire

WITH SO MUCH IN SCRIPTURE POINTING US to the Day of the LORD, and admonitions like "he who endures to the end will be saved,"[1] we are not left to wonder whether we work till the end of this age and give account for it all in the beginning of the next. Yet in doing so, we mustn't lose sight of the *next*. There is an age to come—in fact, there are many.[2] We have so much to look forward to in eternity with Jesus and our Father. This present age is much like an investment into all that is to come, affecting our assignment, rank, and influence in the restoration of all things.[3] What we say and do before Jesus' earthly inauguration *really* matters.

But He is not a hard taskmaster, and we are not to become workaholics, however holy or noble the job. If our theology does not produce a tender heart, we're missing something important about who God is and what it means for us in the day-to-day. When we are tired, He gives us rest.[4] When we are burning out, He guards our weak and withering flame.[5] When all is said and done, when everything is revealed, no one will be able to accuse Him of abusive leadership.

1 See Matthew 24:13
2 See Ephesians 2:7
3 See Luke 19:11-27
4 See Psalm 23:1-3
5 See Isaiah 42:3

We are built to display His glory, but we are not so expendable that He will crush us under the cost of obedience or ministry. That said, it is important we not allow ourselves to fall under the crushing weight of demands in life. The apostle Paul emphasized love above any other contribution,[6] and this is true for our sphere of influence within our family lives and fields, foreign or domestic. If you are a parent, you can give your children all the best and shiny things, but Paul's letter to the Corinthian church asks you if you love them. Are you patient with them? If you are a spouse, are you enduring all the worst and believing all the best for your partner in covenant? If you are a college student with rowdy roommates, are you stingy with your food or do you display the generosity of God with cheerfulness and love in your disposition? Love is a practical, tangible means. Our work is to intervene, to intercede, for those around us.

I am convinced, that for all the demands and all the needs and all the opportunities to love and minister and serve, the challenge of our hearts throughout the rest of this age is not primarily to love ourselves and our neighbor. That is a secondary challenge. The challenge of our hearts in this age is to love our Maker, our Husband,[7] and no other. This means our families—or lack thereof—are not our idols. This means our children's well-being is not more important to us than our own lives in God. This means our marriages are not a broken record of Jerry Maguire's codependent "you had me at hello." This means our positions, platforms, and pulpits do not define our failure or success. This means God and God alone is our voice of affirmation. Just as He loves the financial gift given with a happy heart,[8] so He loves the service, devotion, and adoration of a covenantally committed spouse. We can keep our grumpy money, and we can keep our grumpy service.

My gravest warning for a pioneer (though this applies to any believer) is the hazard of duty without beauty. If Jesus Himself needed to withdraw from crowds to be with His Father, and could not manage a ministry of relief and humanitarian aid without a plumb line of prayer, we certainly cannot either, and should not try. Why intentionally discover what will destroy us? Life makes it too easy to distract us

---

6 See Romans 13:8-10; 1 Corinthians 13:13
7 See Isaiah 54:5
8 2 Corinthians 9:7

from who we are made to be, Who we are made in the image of, and what we are ultimately meant to be doing. How many laborers are really just older brothers who spent their whole lives serving their Father, and fundamentally forgot or overlooked who He really is? Do we want to be with *Him*, or do we just want access to all His stuff and good steaks?

If you take a blue highlighter through the New Testament and color in all the things the Word tells us God did and does for us in Christ—theologians call these "indicatives"—you will find your Gospels and epistles become oceans. I really do encourage you to do this. Follow this practice with a green highlighter for "imperatives"—what we're then commanded to do—and you'll find islands dotting these seas of God's incredible and unwavering goodness towards us in Jesus. If you've been serving Him for years, do this and remember. If you've never done this before, do it now and wonder. If you've just come to Jesus…welcome to the party.

What we find in Scripture is not emotional manipulation or doctrinal bullying to spend our lives in the service of King Jesus. We find we *get* to serve Him because we *get* to know Him because we *get* to love Him. All our days and duties are to be grounded in loving Him. He calls this "abiding in the Vine."[9] We know we've stopped abiding when we get mad that the little brother gets a party with the fattened calf, or begin to wonder wistfully about the life that could have been. I know what it is to question the worth of Jesus and resent the Great Commission. Sometimes, all it takes to push me over the edge is to run out of good coffee a continent away from the nearest cafe. (This probably means coffee is my idol.)

We love Him *because* He first loved us.[10] We see Him *because* He enlightened us. We serve Him *because* He equipped us. Sometimes assignments and deployments take their toll, and we need to retreat "under the shade of the apple tree"[11] for a while. It will take our lifetimes to learn the depths of what it means to love Jesus, but He gave us something of a "Love God 101" in His final conversations before His crucifixion: obey Me. Loving Jesus means obeying Jesus.

---

9   John 15:1-10
10 1 John 4:19
11 See Song of Solomon 8:5

Obedient disciples cherish Jesus' name above their own. Obedient disciples make disciples, serving newcomers to this holy family with stewardship of the gifts given to them by the grace of God[12]—it is not ours to "convert." It is ours to serve.

Affection-based obedience infuses our work with joy, our relationships with patience, our decisions with peace, our behavior with self-control, our integrity with faithfulness, our responses with kindness, our rebukes with gentleness, our character with goodness, and our disposition with love.[13] Every law and commandment's bottom line is that which is patient, kind, long-suffering, humble, meek, burden-bearing, and encouraging. A life of obedience is a life yoked to the Lord's, deciding every day to not abuse the privilege of being given His name, lest we take it in vain.[14]

Paul's work to proclaim Christ where He's never been heard of before was a means and method of his apostolic burden to guard the core and lay the right foundation for the Church to be built upon worldwide. In his first letter to the Corinthians, he addressed the principle of multiple contributions to the global effort—using their community as an example. In our own lives, and in our own ministries and communities, someone will sow seeds, someone else will water the soil, and someone else will help reap the harvest. Why does the Lord do it this way? Will it not get confusing or convoluted? Not if we "take care how we build" on the only legitimate foundation, which is Christ and Him crucified.[15] In fact, this kind of unified effort serves to grow the corporate body of Jesus into full maturity.[16] It may seem like we have a long way to go, but take heart—Jesus finishes what He starts.

One sobering truth that cannot be glossed over is this: the Day will reveal what kind of work it was.[17] Meaning, we can all be under one impression of a ministry's legitimacy, and find out when the Lord issues judgments and decrees that we were altogether mistaken. As we work, we are not to labor in vain. Who wants to spend their whole life building a ministry empire so it can collapse on the Day of the

---

12 See Matthew 28:18-20; Ephesians 4:7
13 Galatians 5:22-23
14 Exodus 20:7; Deuteronomy 5:11; Psalm 139:20
15 See Romans 15:18-21; 1 Corinthians 2:2; 3:9-15
16 Ephesians 4:11-16
17 See 1 Corinthians 3:13

LORD? Who wants to serve their own interests or stroke their own egos so it can all be devoured by fire? Nobody. No sane person wants to watch their life disintegrate as we cross the threshold into eternity. Nobody wants to look at Jesus and regret what we did or didn't do, though surely nearly all of us will stand in the shadow of some kind of regret. He will graciously vanquish even those,[18] but why abuse His generosity to excuse shirking of our own responsibility? Who doesn't want a pile of gold to stack at His feet in the better Bethlehem, and be a wise man standing before the greater manger?[19]

He is not unfair or unjust and as such, will not forget even our slightest measure of obedience, our smallest sacrifice.[20] He will remember even a glass of water we give to someone who is thirsty—*in His name*. It is an important qualification. Service in anyone else's name—including our own—will burn in the fire of that great and terrible Day. This can be real water to satiate literal dehydration, or water that has a life of its own, the good news of His glorious grace.[21] He sees and remembers and will honor everything we ever say and ever do. He'll never forget the legitimate things we say no to, so we can turn to Him instead. He is a good Father who knows our frame, knows we are but dust, knows we have a measured capacity, and knows first-hand that life in this age isn't always easy. He is generous in His remembrance—just ask Sarah.[22] When He reveals every thought, action, intent, and will, "each one's praise will come from God,"[23] which allows us to rest easy as we work. We're not here to impress the people we serve. We're not here to prove ourselves to ourselves, or our parents or community. We're just here to make much of the Name that's better than all the others, and feel His smile on our lives as we do.

---

18 Romans 8:1
19 See Matthew 2:1-11; Revelation 4:10-5:14
20 See Hebrews 6:10
21 See John 4:10,13-14; Ephesians 1:6
22 See Genesis 18:10-15; Hebrews 11:11
23 1 Corinthians 4:5

CHAPTER TWENTY-SEVEN

A Unique Confrontation

IN 1839, A PARTY FROM THE LONDON MISSIONARY SOCIETY came ashore on an island in the chain, then called the New Hebrides (now Vanuatu). They arrived to bring the Gospel to the island's native residents, two centuries after Europeans began engaging with the South Pacific on trade routes. Within minutes, John Williams and James Harris were met and immediately speared by the locals whose shores they'd just intruded upon. They were then eaten. The tribes were cannibalistic.

Members of their party managed to escape and lived to tell the tale. As word reached Queen Victoria's kingdom, the British public was mortified that such an undignified and horrific fate could befall their well-intentioned missionaries. Evangelistic efforts in the South Pacific dried up pretty quickly. The New Hebrides were left without a Gospel witness, condemned for their depraved brutality.

John G. Paton was fifteen at the time. After graduating university, he took on a role as a missionary in inner-city Glasgow and served well in a legitimate, noble, and challenging domestic ministry post. Yet, as years passed, he became increasingly burdened that no one was returning to the New Hebrides. "[Those islands] were baptized with the blood of the martyrs, and Christ thereby told the whole Christian world that He claimed these islands as His own."[1] He reasoned that if he left his post in Glasgow, forty young men would line up to take his place—but nobody was sailing to the New Hebrides. Unable to shake the conviction to go, he began to make plans.

All but his parents opposed him. In particular, a certain older gentleman in the missions society would persistently challenge John to keep his job and stay put. There were many good reasons why: faithfulness, stewardship, thriving success. Paton held his ground. Their conversations would always become heated enough that the older man would burst out what Paton called his "crowning argument." Flustered, the man would exclaim: "The cannibals! You will be eaten by cannibals!"

The anxious gentleman's misplaced concern for Paton's preservation was met with an impossibly gracious and clearly convicted response: "Mr. Dickson," said the young man bound for the islands; "You are advanced in years now, and your own prospect is soon to be laid in the grave, there to be eaten by worms; I confess to you, that if I can but live and die serving and honoring the Lord Jesus, it will make no difference to me whether I am eaten by Cannibals or by worms; and in the Great Day my Resurrection body will rise as fair as yours in the likeness of our risen Redeemer."[2]

With the remaining unreached and unengaged people groups largely concentrated across the Arab and Muslim worlds, it is no longer cannibals people fear. It is jihadis. Nobody wants to get beheaded on YouTube. Nobody wants their mother to watch their moment of martyrdom. Nobody wants that to happen to anybody.

Fear and self-preservation are bad reasons to white-knuckle the name of Jesus.

Just as Hudson Taylor became "unable to bear the sight of a thousand or more Christian people rejoicing in their own security, while millions were perishing for lack of knowledge,"[3] we must become unable to bear the sight of Gospel-saturation in the West while *billions* perish for lack of the saving knowledge of Jesus. If we hold the saving

---

1 Paton, J.G. *John G. Paton: Missionary to the New Hebrides, An Autobiography Edited by His Brother* (1965, orig. 1889). Edinburgh: The Banner of Truth Trust. p. 75.

2 Paton, John G. *John G. Paton: Missionary to the New Hebrides, An Autobiography Edited by His Brother*, (1889). p. 56.

3 Piper, John. "The Ministry of Hudson Taylor," (2014). Accessed July 2018. http://www.desiringgod.org/messages/the-ministry-of-hudson-taylor-as-life-in-christ.

knowledge of Jesus, we are stewards of the saving knowledge of Jesus. We might read Romans 1:14 and think it only applies to Paul. It doesn't. If we have the Gospel of the Kingdom, we're under obligation to it. It begins to bear upon us the moment truth first illuminates light in the dark of our godless hearts.

A chaplain walked a despised criminal to the gallows of London in 1879, reading from *The Consolations of Religion*. The condemned, a thief and murderer named Charles Peace, exclaimed: "Sir, if I believed what you and the church of God say that you believe, even if England were covered with broken glass from coast to coast, I would walk over it, if need be, on hands and knees and think it worthwhile living, just to save one soul from an eternal hell like that!"[4]

It should not surprise us that a man facing death would hear the news of the Kingdom with more urgency and sobriety than most of us feel in our lifetimes of comfortable and uncostly discipleship. But we cannot avoid or ignore the knowledge of the billions breathing on the earth right now who've not heard about Jesus. At a minimum, the hemorrhaging crises in the Middle East and North Africa prove we can remove unprecedented suffering from the realm of impossibilities. They press our own nationalism, sometimes revealing it to exist to begin with: are we more concerned with the peace and prosperity of our birth nation and personal empire, or are we willing to go to dark and difficult places simply to serve them with the name of their Maker? Is it enough for us that Jesus isn't receiving worship in many nations across the earth, that are His by divine right and inheritance? Does it bother us just enough that He deserves a witness (people's responses to the Gospel being between them and their Maker) that we'll provide it for them? Is He worth it? Do they deserve it?

Some of the people I serve alongside can point to a moment in their history when they felt the Lord say something like "embrace the Middle East." I've never had that moment. But because of their obedience, I was presented with opportunities and decisions alike. I could drop them off at the airport, or I could get on the plane with them. It is a longer story, but I ended up getting on the plane; not because I'm burdened by statistics and figures, but because it bothers

---

[4] Ravenhill, Leonard. *Why Revival Tarries* (1987; orig. 1959). Bloomington: Bethany House. p. 33-34.

me that ears made by Jesus have never heard of Jesus. Statistics have their place, but for however valid and indicting they are, they do not move me enough to put my mother through what I have put her through. I'm not asking for them to move you either.

The witness that Jesus is our prize—above every career ambition, relationship, and financial goal—is the only witness He deserves. Life offers a lot of stuff—legitimate and otherwise—but He is our "exceedingly great reward," for Whom to live is life itself, and by Whom death brings our most precious gain.[5] Paul highlighted this when he wrote of marriage and singleness in light of ministry and the return of the Lord; let no thing or person become an idol barring you from wholehearted devotion to Jesus, knowing the bridge between your birthday and the end of the age is shorter than we realize.[6] At the end of everything, our witness to the remaining unreached has been that we simply don't think Jesus is worth moving there to declare. He isn't worth the cultural confusion. He isn't worth the language barrier. He isn't worth the danger. He isn't worth the cost.

Years after escaping Irish slavery, a young man named Patrick was a bishop in his homeland. By his own confession, he had been a pagan son of fourth-century Romans Catholic parents when the Irish raiders robbed him of his family, household, inheritance, and future. His education was aborted, and his literacy and Latin never fully recovered.[7] He was born the privileged son of a nobleman, only to be consigned to working someone else's property, caring for the sheep on someone else's farm, a slave to the benefit of someone else's fortune. It was on long, rainy days on those emerald hills he turned to the God of his father and grandfather, and carved out a prayer life in this pagan land of brutes and barbarians. He was already one of the first witnesses of the Gospel in Ireland—nobody had bothered to cross the Irish Sea with the Good News yet. Nobody from Rome wanted to go.

---

5 See Genesis 15:1; Matthew 5:12; Luke 6:23,35; Philippians 1:21; Hebrews 10:35; 11:26
6 See 1 Corinthians 7:1-31
7 There are a number of biographies written about Patrick; some provide better historical and cultural synopses and contexts than others. But to hear his story, begin with the works he penned himself: *My Name is Patrick* and *Confession*. Both are available on Kindle.

Patrick had not long returned home when he had a dream of the Irish begging him to return.[8] "O holy boy, come and walk amongst us once more!" Victoricus stood before him, with a letter from the Irish. As he recorded this experience, he was faced with once again leaving his home and family—this time voluntarily—to live amongst the people considered to be the scum of the earth. The Irish were despised by Romans, and Brits didn't think any higher of them. With an established ministry and assigned post, Patrick had more than a few reasons to shake off the dream and refuse to go. Even with a commissioning dream, he took stock of his life and thought through his list of pros and cons; reasons to go, reasons to stay. I believe many of us simply need to follow Patrick's lead, and take an inventory of our lives. What keeps us from packing our bags? What keeps us at home? How do these reasons compete with what would compel us to "go and make disciples"?[9]

When my friends told me they were moving to the Middle East, I had a similar experience to Patrick (except that I've never had that kind of a dream). He said when he laid it all out and wrote it all down, he had "no reason to go, save for the Gospel and God's promises."[10] Whatever was on his list of reasons to stay, the Gospel and God's integrity were enough for him to go. They proved to be reason enough for me as well.

This man gave himself to this pagan land so entirely, we forget he wasn't actually Irish. His mother did not call him "Patrick," certainly not "Paddy," and for centuries, *nobody* believed that a drunken parade and green fountain was an appropriate way to honor him. This pioneering man went to the known ends of his earth simply for the fame of the name, simply because the Gospel mattered more than his own life, and effectively mobilized teams of others to do the same. This son of British Rome baptized princesses and paupers alike, picked fights with deluded kings, and preached the Gospel to wicked men wearing tiny crowns simply because he had learned something of enemy love, of "Calvary love,"[11] that placed his own life and dreams

---

8   St Patrick. *My Name is Patrick* (Kindle Locations 114-122). Royal Irish Academy. Kindle Edition.
9   Matthew 28:19
10 St Patrick. *My Name is Patrick* (Kindle Locations 309-311). Royal Irish Academy.
11 See Amy Carmichael's work of this title

squarely beneath the sake of others, and far below the sake of the name of Jesus.

These early decades of this millennium are unique, and many global events and tragedies uniquely confront our priorities and ambitions. Will we choose safety and security over the fame of Jesus? Will we white-knuckle what isn't ours to hold? Will we do all we can to break age-old bonds over nations and cultures with the liberating truth of Him who is Truth? Or will we respond to a unique opportunity in a unique hour of history the way that Jonah did—clutching our own values, dreams, and national borders? Whose legacy will we live for—ours or the LORD's?

> *When I come to die*
>
> *O when I come to die*
>
> *When I come to die*
>
> *Give me Jesus.*

CHAPTER TWENTY-EIGHT

Elevating or Emulating

THE MAN TASKED WITH BRINGING THE GOSPEL to the Gentiles was not the first man to engage in long-term cross-cultural ministry, but he is certainly the most well-known and perhaps the most accomplished. Paul covered territory like he needed passport stamps to prove he did the job. We are encouraged to "imitate him as he imitated Christ,"[1] but I cannot find a single verse where Paul or even another apostle explicitly and expressly recruited people to become missionaries. He simply prioritized Jesus, love for Jesus, obedience to Jesus (the Lord would likely say those are one and the same)[2] and trusted Jesus. Certainly, we are to pray to the Lord of the Harvest to send laborers, and should probably be something less than surprised to find He decides to send us.[3] But I do not think either Paul or Jesus would try to brow-beat somebody into fulfilling the Great Commission.

Some offense at some missional rhetoric has kept people from considering it as a call—and many have used the excuse of poor recruitment tactics to spurn the call. The Lord has plans and dreams for all our lives individually—but we are called, unequivocally, to exalt

---
1   See 1 Corinthians 11:1
2   See Deuteronomy 6:1-4; Matthew 22:36-40
3   See Luke 10:2-3

Jesus in everything.[4] Doing that job well demands we meet the needs presented by Gospel poverty throughout all nations and our communities. This will require a deep and mutually honoring relationship between the Pauls of pioneering and the Timothys of Ephesus, just as the brothers in the Bible served and encouraged each other. What we cannot get away with is cloaking ambivalent irresponsibility under the guise of "being missional everywhere"—as though we actually do intentionally preach the Gospel in our hometowns or diligently share Jesus with strangers at Starbucks. If at the end of the day we think things on the home front are shinier and better than the glory of Jesus where He's presently receiving no glory, let's just call it what it is. If we're happy living under the bondage of sin and would prefer not to see the Son of Man come in all His glory to right every wrong, let's just admit we have our own priorities and dreams. But let's not claim to love Jesus "above all else."

The missionary endeavor has been understaffed and underfunded probably since Jesus ascended from the Mount of Olives. That's not on a fast track to change, but it could before He comes. I'm not unreasonably pessimistic or cynical. In my observation, much of our general lack of participation—going or sending—in the Great Commission is a result of ignorance of the beauty of Jesus. Either we really do think other pursuits are better pursuits, or we don't think we're qualified. But we're qualified.[5] We need training and discipleship and wisdom to execute an intelligent plan to engage a different culture, but we also just need Jesus. It's not impossible, and it's not difficult. The "apostle to the Gentiles" started out as a Type A zealot so committed to the status quo that he took lives in cold blood to maintain it. If we elevate Paul to an inaccessible realm of "super Christian," we will never emulate Paul. Scripture encourages us to emulate Paul.[6]

When you read Paul's descriptions of Jesus, or that "all is loss, Christ is life, death is gain,"[7] can you identify with and relate to what he discovered about Jesus that changed everything for him? Or does it intimidate you? Or does it confound you?

What if you could find and feel the magnificence of Jesus just like

---
4   See Colossians 1:9,18
5   See Colossians 1:12
6   See 1 Corinthians 11:1
7   Philippians 1:21

Paul did? What if "abiding in the vine"[8] began to look like bankrupting your life and time and energy and resources to make His name known—and you enjoyed it? If Christ be anything, He must be everything.[9] I'm inclined to think some nations remain unreached, because those that already have been are full of Christians living tragically beneath the intentions of God for our lives. It is "life and life abundant"[10]—even with incredible suffering—or bust. He is who He says He is, or we can all go home.

Something tremendous occurred in Paul, this former Pharisee and bloodthirsty "once was,"[11] that wrought in him the unwavering conviction that "to live is Christ, and death is gain."[12] To "live" meant emulating the King who bled out between criminals so His enemies could survive guilt and see innocence. To die meant to be with that humble Man forever. Fire forged that conviction within him; it may have been a slow burn, or perhaps it was the only thing he knew he could see straight after glory blinded him.[13] What I know is this: he yoked himself to Jesus, and grace never let him deviate back to depravity.[14] He went all in. Paul was a son of Abraham if there ever was one: If God be anything, He is the God who raises the dead. Paul clung to the LORD of the resurrection.

Make decisions that only make sense if you'll be raised from the dead.[15]

---

8   See John 15:1-9
9   Spurgeon, Charles H., "Christ is All" (1871). Accessed July 2018. http://www.spurgeon.org/sermons/1006.php.
10 See Isaiah 55:1-11; John 10:10
11 See Romans 11:30; 1 Corinthians 6:11; Galatians 1:23; Ephesians 2:3,13; 5:8; Colossians 1:21; Titus 3:3; 1 Peter 3:20
12 Philippians 1:21
13 See Acts 9:1-16
14 See 2 Corinthians 12:9
15 I believe this phrase is attributed to John Piper.

CHAPTER TWENTY-NINE

THE WISEST WASTE

PERHAPS THE DEATH AND RESURRECTION of Lazarus is a familiar story. If it isn't, you'll find it in the eleventh chapter of John's record of Jesus' life and ministry. Not far from Jerusalem was a small town called Bethany. Jesus spent significant time there, both quantitatively and qualitatively, with a small family of three grown siblings: two sisters and a brother.

If you're not an only child, you'll identify with their family dynamics. We don't know much about Lazarus, but we know Martha was the responsible sister, and Mary was the "dancer." (I'm the second of four kids, so consider this my self-disclosed bias.) They had Jesus and His massive, frat-house-entourage over for at least one meal before Lazarus died (likely several more, considering their relational equity expressed in the texts),[1] and Martha did all the work. Thirteen or more men, hungry from walking around in the blistering sun and ministering to demanding crowds, are in their living room with whomever else in town was invited over to meet the Messiah, and a Middle Eastern meal is readied for a Viking-sized table. One woman was in the kitchen.

One.

---
1 See Luke 10:38-42; John 11:1-44

Martha gets a bad rap and a lot of heat now in sermons, but I think she's an easy target. Who wouldn't be stressed out over making sure Jesus had the best hospitality experience possible? I would be. Would I need to be? No. I'd be every kind of disarmed and uncomfortable with His ease, but I'd still be Martha in the kitchen. I'm Martha in my life. I get it. So I understand that when she's overwhelmed, she cries out to the LORD: "Don't You care that I'm alone here? Don't You care that my lazy sister is in the living room with a bunch of men, defying all our cultural standards, breaching all our protocol, listening to You talk while I'm in here making sure all you frat boys are fed?"[2]

Imagine how many jaws dropped—Martha's included—when He said, "Martha, of course I care, but you assumed I assigned you there. That's culture. That ain't Jesus. I appreciate everything you're doing, but if anyone needs to choose between serving Me and sitting with Me, it's isn't your sister. It's you."[3]

So these siblings got front-row seats and experiential evidence to life-changing revelations about Jesus you and I are still chewing on.

He would rather go hungry than be alone.

Does He need us?

No.

Does He need food?

Definitely not.[4]

So what does He want?

We need to understand something; and I would say, those of us in a vocational ministry that makes a 9-to-5 out of serving Jesus really need to understand something about Jesus: He does not need you. He does not need your food. He does not need your massive meal spread out on the table. He wants you, and you need Him and all the Bread of Life that He is[5] like your next breath depends on it. But you also need to want Him, or you won't abide in the Vine.[6] Instead, you'll eventually begin to resent Him. You'll begin to believe

---

2   Luke 10:40
3   Luke 10:41-42
4   See Psalm 50:12
5   See John 6:35,48,51
6   See John 15

His yoke is difficult rather than easy, and His burden heavy rather than light.[7] And if you don't let Him illuminate the resentment early enough, your heart will callous over—and a calloused heart always leads to a seared conscience, whether you're up to your eyeballs in brazen sin or not. Short of intervention, a seared conscience will bury you and people you love along with all your good works, and you will discover in no less than swift terms how quickly a house of cards can fall. Consider David, who left an intact town for work one morning only to discover everything in an ash heap when he came home for dinner.[8]

You will, over the course of your life, spend evenings at His feet hanging on His every Word. Those are evenings well spent. You will also, over the course of your life, spend evenings working into the twilight hours doing a great work. Those are good efforts. When you're doing a great work, don't come down[9]—except to do what Mary did, and return again to the presence and teachings and life and vibrancy of intimacy with Jesus. And if you ever have to choose between the two, and find yourself prioritizing work over Word, check yourself before you wreck yourself. And consider the fruit borne from the two trees illustrated by these two women's lives:

Eventually, their brother died.[10] It sounds like a sudden sickness took him out, though they expected him to reach the end of his lifespan. Both women understood Jesus' presence could've stopped death from taking their brother. Both heard Him declare, either in person or by testimony, that He is more than just a bouncer who checks death at the door—He is the resurrection's LORD.[11] Meaning He doesn't just supervise the power that pulls men out of the grave, He governs it. Martha took courage that one day—"one day"—she'd see her brother again. I am sure it edified her and emboldened her confidence in Jesus. It was not fruitless. It likely would have carried her through grief if her brother hadn't been extracted from the tomb later that day. Mary, though, wept at the LORD of the Resurrection's feet—before watching Him execute unmatched authority over both the sickness

---

7 See Matthew 11
8 See 1 Samuel 30:1-3
9 See Nehemiah 6:3
10 See John 11
11 John 11:25

that robbed her brother's strength, and the decay that met him in the grave with a few simple words. Jesus likely had to specify that only Lazarus "come out"[12] that day, lest every tomb in earshot open up to release their inhabitants.

Something lodged in Mary.[13] Something clicked and crystallized and began to make sense of everything she'd heard Jesus talk about at length, mention over dinner, add as an aside or quip in a conversation. I can't say with certainty when this happened, but I'm guessing (for a few informed reasons) it was around the time she was unwrapping her brother's burial clothes. The Spirit of revelation revealed something to her: the LORD of the Resurrection Himself would see a resurrection.

Which meant He had to die.

Jesus was going to die.

This had to have kept her up at night.

Responding to Revelation
"The LORD will provide Himself the lamb."[14] Abraham did not lie, but heaven only provided a ram the day Isaac was spared—but He had promised a Lamb. The One who opened deaf ears and healed blind eyes and restored lame bodies and did crazy things with food and brought her dead brother back to life was going to die. Who could have handled that kind of information without being destroyed by it? Everyone in Bethany was offended Jesus didn't show up soon enough to keep Lazarus alive. Several mocked Him when He did arrive, that He'd somehow met His match. The LORD does not give precious pearls to irreverent swine.[15] He trusted Mary with the holy heads-up that He was about to lay His life on the altar of Moriah, and she had a heart to hear it because she had been listening. She hadn't taken for granted the privilege to be near Him and hear Him. Even His disciples, who were in-between squabbles over who was the best disciple and most qualified for the most power and authority, had

---

12   John 11:43
13   I'm speculating as to when/how/why she received this revelation, but she did receive it and responded in like kind.
14   Genesis 22:8
15   Matthew 7:6

missed the clear implications of blatant hints and outright declarations concerning His coming crucifixion.

Mary didn't miss it.

And she knew she had to do something.

The next time she saw Jesus, she did something.

Once again, everyone's in the living room. Lazarus is there, presumably enjoying not being dead. Martha's probably still the only one making sure there's food on the table, but hopefully her heart is a little softer and a bit more glad than it was the last we saw her. All the boys are there. Judas is there, his pockets lined with robberies out of their ministry money box. Everyone's there, and everyone's got an opinion about this young, unmarried sister in the Bethany family. When she emerges, she's carrying forty grand in her arms.[16]

Scholars and historians speculate a few reasons why a young woman with no mentioned living parents in a dusty outpost town would have the luxury of an alabaster jar full of costly perfume worth a year's wages. It could've been her inheritance, or her dowry set aside for when a suitor would come. It could've been a few things when it came to her, but once she had it, without question, it was her future.

And then she broke it.

Intentionally.

She didn't trip. She didn't accidentally spill it. She walked right up to Jesus and poured it all over Him. The audacity of this girl! What if He didn't want it? What did she know about Him that made her so sure she could keep getting away with defying social order and culture and family protocol and whatever else? Whatever she knew, I need to know it too. I need to know Jesus that well.

The room erupted. Judas balked. "What a waste! *Why this waste?!* You stupid girl! If you wanted to do something noble, exercise some wisdom! We could have sold this and fed every hungry person in the country for a year! What is your problem?! Why do you keep doing such stupid stuff?"

John makes a point to tell us Judas wasn't concerned for the poor.

---

16 Conventional speculation among scholars is that this amounted to a year's worth of wages (three hundred denarii; see John 12:5).

He was mad this was three hundred less denarii that he had access to for his own greed.[17] Nevertheless, do not stop at Judas' sin and gloss over the fact that every leader in the Christian movement is in the room and one of them—who was a pretty dicey character—made one appeal to social justice over an extravagant display of worship, and every other apostolic leader agreed. No one wanted to be the guy who didn't defend the poor. But nobody affirmed or valued appropriate worship of and devotion to Jesus.

Consider that. Consider the priority of good works and social justice in our cultural theology. Consider it when you hear "preach the Gospel; use words if necessary." When you jog through your Twitter feed. When humanitarian organizations run by people who know the name of Jesus orchestrate entire operations to hand out literal water without prioritizing Living Water, and you wonder if you should sink money into their work. Let us not make idols of money or reputation. Let us not give them the thrones of our hearts. Let us never prioritize fleeting things over the preeminence of our King.

Judas' public offense and the disciples' corporate objection to Mary's extravagance is less than a week before Jesus would be killed. It's something like three years after He plucked them out of obscurity, gave them a ministry platform, flipped their worldview upside down, and taught them one-on-one about the Kingdom of God.

They still didn't think He was worth that kind of reckless abandonment.

This is what pushed Judas to sell Jesus for thirty silver coins.[18]

Mary saw Him now and then, and she knew He was worth more than some pocket change. And she knew her time was running out. John's account of her extravagant display comes one chapter after he tells us about Lazarus coming out of the grave. God dropped something in Mary's gut, and she responded appropriately to the urgency she felt. She knew Jesus' days were numbered. She knew hers were as well. She wasn't going to miss her shot to give Him everything she had.

Once again, Jesus silences the room with one rebuke. Once again, He publicly affirms Mary's devotion. To the offended men in the room, He retorted, "Why do you bother her? Leave her alone. She just did

---

17 John 12:6
18 Matthew 26:16

something good to Me for My burial. You will always have humanitarian needs to serve and mercy ministries to run. You will not always have Me. These days are numbered, boys. You had an opportunity, and she took it. Don't despise her for it. In fact, tell everyone about this. When you tell them about Me, tell them about her."[19]

Water From Bethlehem's Well
When David first began to run from Saul, he ended up hiding in a cave called Adullam. For several years. All kinds of rumors were swirling about him; it was a complicated time in his life. What is not complicated is that four hundred men joined him there—men who were in debt, distress, or discontent[20]—and David began to lead them. I'm glossing over so many important issues surrounding David's leadership, character, trials, tests, responses, humility, and teachability—but the significant point here is every one of those four hundred men could've served Saul instead. He was the sure bet. He had the throne. He also had a horrible temper, jealousy issues, unpredictable outbursts, and a penchant for blatant disobedience. Some of these men probably just needed a place to be, but eventually saw something in how the future king carried himself with wisdom while hiding from the present king in a cave. My guess is they realized 'you are who you hang out with.' I think not a few of them wanted to become good men. They wanted to be men like David.

Years later, long after Saul died, long after ascensions, long after recklessly sinful decisions, long after mutinies, long after mercies, David and his men found themselves again fighting the Philistines.[21] The battle brought them near David's hometown, and he craved a glass of water from Bethlehem's well. Its source spring was just over the battle line. His dearest buddies heard his pipe dream, and they hatched a plan. In the middle of active war, they were going to sneak across enemy lines, find the well, get some water, and bring it back to their king. Because they loved him. Because it was extravagant. Because it wasn't about water.

They did it. They pulled it off, survived, and managed to get the water back to this man they'd served and loved and followed for so

---
19 See Matthew 26:6-13; John 12:1-8
20 1 Samuel 22:1-2
21 2 Samuel 23:13-17

many years. When they emerged from enemy lines with the desire of his heart—however petty it might have seemed—he couldn't believe it. And he couldn't drink it. He poured it out to the LORD. It soaked the ground that could've been soaked with their blood for the risk of their attempt.

Because it wasn't about water.

"It is for freedom Christ has set us free,"[22] and it is our liberty to lavish our love upon the Lover of our souls. We don't know what our window of opportunity looks like, but we do know our days are numbered and this age is all we have to lay our lives down. All the lights are on once He comes back. We get all our rewards and confront all our regrets when He returns.[23] He will not be unjust to forget even the smallest and slightest act of obedience and devotion.[24] Right now, we're soldiers.[25] Right now, it's wartime. And we only have one life. One jar to smash. One shot to cross enemy lines to get the water out of the well.

Would we not take it?

An Appropriately Fragrant Death

Mary's security would've soaked into Jesus' skin and hair so deep, no shower could have scrubbed it away for weeks. Her perfume saturated Him. Maybe people thought it made Him smell a little bit like a girl for a while. I don't think He cared. He knew it smelled like worship. And He knew it was right.

Mary may not have known quite how quickly He'd face what she anointed Him for, but she definitely knew it would have been inappropriate for Him to face the cross without it. She knew it would have been inappropriate for Jesus to get lashed without ever having been lavished upon. She knew her days were dwindling to hours. And she gave Him everything she had to offer.

When He did get lashed—just a few days later—He would have still smelled like the inheritance Mary so wisely wasted on Him. Every time His skin was struck, everyone around would have smelled the

---

[22] Galatians 5:1
[23] See Revelation 22:12
[24] Hebrews 6:10
[25] See Philippians 2:25; 2 Timothy 2:1-4; Philemon 1:2

copper in His blood mingled with the decision Mary made to love Him well. Every time He inhaled, He would have smelled not just her inheritance, but His as well: the exceeding love of one "forgiven much."[26] The appropriately extravagant worship from every tribe, tongue, people, and nation.[27] The equally yoked, equally mature bride made ready. The wife of the Lamb, shaped from His pierced side. The affection from His bride that did not say no when it inconvenienced her, who did not run for the hills when loving well cost her something beautiful.

When He was hoisted into the air, held by rusty and rugged nails to splintered planks of now blood-soaked wood. He would have smelled like the night He got dinner at a leper named Simon's house, when a young girl laid her life on the line to prepare Him to lay His on the altar. I'm confident she didn't regret it then. I've wondered if she ever felt the pain of liquidating her life's financial security at such a young age when she was, say, forty. Sixty. Eighty-five. If it was her dowry, was she then single until she died? What would that have felt like in that age and culture? Did the devil ever come to her and whisper "Why this waste?" in her ear? Did she ever wonder if she could have perhaps done something a little less costly to make the point? When life's cruelties confronted her youthful zeal, did she have any regrets?

My guess is all she'd have to remember was the voice of Judas, and the voice of Jesus. By the end of the week, one man was hanging from a tree by his neck and the Other was hanging from a tree by His hands and feet. I doubt she ever questioned the wisdom of her decision… But many of us will. Many of us will decide early on in our lives to waste them on Jesus. Then we'll wake up when we're thirty and wonder if we're making the right decisions. We'll wake up in our mid-forties and wonder if it's still worth it. If He is still worth it. We might ask ourselves when we're old enough to be grandparents if there is still wisdom in our waste.

I'm confident if Mary could take you out for coffee and sit across from you at the table, she'd lean in, look you in the eye and tell you, with everything she knew that night in Bethany and knows now in eternity, to bust your alabaster wide open and let every drop fall on

---

26   Luke 7:47
27   See Revelation 5:9; 7:9

the One we will fall on our knees before. Let your livelihood and securities and sureties soak themselves into your only true hope, and cling to Him so closely that you begin to then carry His fragrance with you everywhere you go. Find the break in the enemy line and get the water from Bethlehem's well. When the sun sets on this age and rises on the next, you will not find yourself harboring any bitter regrets.

Let your life be Christ.

Let your death be gain.

Because this isn't about water.

It's about Jesus.

Appendix
I Never Made a Sacrifice

"For my own part, I have never ceased to rejoice that God has appointed me to such an office. People talk of the sacrifice I have made in spending so much of my life in Africa. Can that be called a sacrifice which is simply paid back as a small part of a great debt owing to our God, which we can never repay? Is that a sacrifice which brings its own blest reward in healthful activity, the consciousness of doing good, peace of mind, and a bright hope of a glorious destiny hereafter? Away with the word in such a view, and with such a thought! It is emphatically no sacrifice. Say rather it is a privilage.

Anxiety, sickness, suffering, or danger, now and then, with a foregoing of the common conveniences and charities of this life, may make us pause, and cause the spirit to waver, and the soul to sink, but let this only be for a moment. All these are nothing when compared with the glory which shall hereafter be revealed in and for us. I never made a sacrifice."

David Livingstone, Pioneer to Africa

ACKNOWLEDGMENTS

Devon Phillips and Gabrielle Prose gave very helpful feedback to the shape of this book. Autumn Crew gave it a thorough and diligent editorial wash and polish. I appreciate all of you taking the time to help craft this into its most beneficial form possible.

Jeff, thanks for swinging the 2x4. Thanks also for sticking around for the aftermath.

Mom, thanks for the courthouse that one time and everything before and after.

D, A, and the rest of our family of cute little blood-bought hobbits: It is the privilege of my life to love and serve King Jesus alongside you. Currahee.

ABOUT THE AUTHOR

Stephanie Quick is a writer and producer serving in the Middle East with Frontier Alliance International and PILGRIM MEDIA. She is the author of *Confronting Unbelief*, *To Trace a Rising Sun*, and the producer of several FAI STUDIOS films, including the *Covenant and Controversy* series. Find out more at **stephaniequick.org**.

ABOUT FAI

Frontier Alliance International is devoted to exalting the worth of Jesus Christ among the unreached and unengaged at the end of the age. For more information on our initiatives serving strategic regions throughout the 10/40 Window, visit **faimission.org**.

Because life is a vapor. Because death is gain. Because obedience. Because "do not take My Name in vain." Because life is Christ. Because faith. Because Gospel. Because it's for His glory's sake. Because the King will return. Because "the greatest of these is love." Because Psalm seventy-two. Because Revelation twenty-one. Because hope. Because this story isn't done. Because we're going to make plowshares out of all our swords and every gun. Because barrel bombs shouldn't fall. Because He took on flesh and blood. Because He said "go tell them all." Because He still does. Because nothing matters more than this. Because every nation needs a witness. Because the unreached deserve it. Because so many haven't heard yet. Because the manger. Because He knelt to wash our feet. Because grace. Because His blood still intercedes. Because the prophecies. Because Jerusalem and "blessed is He." Because it's not because He needs us. Because Zion.

because Jesus.

Made in the USA
Columbia, SC
01 May 2021